Mysterious People of the Bible
In the Light of History

By
Stanley J. St.Clair

Edited by
Michele Doucette

Illustrated by the etchings of the Old Masters

Cover Picture

The Queen of Sheba visits King Solomon, as imagined by 19th century engraver/artist Julius Schnorr von Carolsfeld (1794-1872).

All scriptures are taken from the *King James Version,* except where noted.

ISBN 978-0-9801704-3-6

Printed in the United States of America by
St. Clair Publications
P. O. Box 726
Mc Minnville, TN 37111-0726

http://stan.stclair.net/StClairPublications.html#books
Find us quickly at
http://tinyurl.com/2upgcg

Author's Introduction

Seekers of truth have long questioned the true identity of many mysterious and legendary persons and groups of people introduced in the sacred texts of Judaism and Christianity. In this book, I respectfully present comparisons with various ancient documents, coupled with archeological and DNA evidence, as well as the research of others, both pro and con.

Prejudice is forming opinions, either good or bad, based on insufficient evidence. This work is offered as a challenge for readers to dig deeper into the stories presented in biblical narratives, and draw less biased conclusions based on a greater assemblage of available facts.

Some of the ancient texts used herein include

Antiquities of the Jews and ***Against Apion,*** the writings of Josephus in the first century AD

El-Amarna Letters, Egyptian tablets from the New Kingdom era (1369-1354 BC)

Historia Ecclesiastica, the early Christian Church history of Eusebius of Caesarea (c. 275-339 AD)

Rylands Library Papyrus, dated at 100-175 AD

Quis dives salvabitur, writings of Clement of Alexandria (c.150-211 AD)

The *Qu'ran,* the holy book of Islam

Kebra Negast, the holy writings of Ethiopia

The *Book of Enos*, wholly extant only in the Ethiopic language, usually dated c. 160's BC

The ancient Jewish *Book of Jubilees* (c. 135 BC)

The Jewish rabbinical *Midrash* writings interpreting the Tanakh

The *Babylonian Talmud* (c. 500 CE [AD]) discussion of Jewish customs, ethics, law, and history

The Gnostic *Kabbalah,* work of Jewish mysticism

The *Dead Sea Scrolls*, the sacred writings of the first century AD Essenes of Qumran

The *Royal Canon of Turin,* the best surviving chronology of the ancient Egyptian pharaohs

The *Old Kingdom Pyramid Texts*, of the Egyptian Middle Kingdom (c. 2030-1640 BC)

Coffin Texts, of the Egyptian Middle Kingdom (c. 2030-1640 BC)

The *Book of the Dead* (Egyptian New Kingdom)

The *Papyrus Bremner-Rhind*, containing ancient Egyptian religious beliefs

Contents

I0210719

Chapter One
Cain's Wife, Creationism
And the First Biblical Family

In bygone years, a popular way to spark a lively debate with a student of the Bible was to ask where Cain acquired his wife. Naturally, since it was believed that all humanity sprang from his father, Adam, the first man to be created by God, and his wife, Eve, made from one of his ribs,[1] this dilemma was easily used by skeptics of the scriptures to generate an obstacle to the biblical creation story.

Should this trivial enigma still be an issue today? Or is it even possible that these names merely represent the beginning of mankind, all in keeping with the ancient Hebrew tradition?

Let us begin by first examining the primordial creeds.

According to the fourth chapter of the Book of Genesis, Cain was the first murderer, taking the life of his only brother, Abel (as Seth had not yet been born).[2] For his crime, he was sentenced to become a wanderer, settling in the land of Nod,[3] said to be east of Eden. By mere interpretation, Nod (Hebrew נוד) means "wandering".

Immediately afterward, the text states: "And Cain knew his wife, and she conceived, and bare Enoch: and he builded a city, and called the name of the city after the name of his son, Enoch".[4] No time frame is presented as to how much later the city was built, nor how large a community would qualify to be called a city.

The ancient Jewish *Book of Jubilees* states, "And Cain took 'Âwân his sister to be his wife and she bare him Enoch".[5] By the time Seth would have reached maturity, the *Book of Jubilees* states, "And in the fifth week of the fifth jubilee Seth took 'Azûrâ his sister to be his wife".[6] In Egyptian lore, at least one source states the name of Seth's wife as being Meryet-Nit[7] (see chapter two).

Interestingly enough, biblical students have been in disagreement over the origin of Cain's wife, the most common belief being that the much younger Seth would have taken a mate from the descendants of Cain. Some scholars now believe that there were two creations of man, citing both accounts from Genesis which make mention as to the origin of mankind.[8] In the Bible, much is left open to interpretation, easily giving this impression.

Multiregionalism, another theory, purports that man sprang up in various parts of the world, with no descent from other homo sapiens. This teaching has prevailed among some American first families, as well as the Māori, indigenous peoples of New Zealand, who are thought to have originated in Southeast Asia, migrating from Polynesia. Even tribes such as these have passed down creation legends.

Genealogical DNA findings by Dr. Spencer Wells, in relation to *In Search of Adam*, his TV special, for which I was contacted by the National Geographic Channel, at the request of Niven Sinclair, indicate that the age-old story of all *current* humanity descending from one locale (although seen to have evolved) is true.

In addition, a report published in March 2008 talks of a recent mitochondrial DNA study which suggests that nearly all of the Native Americans currently living in North, Central and South America can trace part of their ancestry to six "founding mothers" whose descendants migrated from Asia around 20,000 years ago.[9]

Given the fact that comparisons of hieroglyphic texts belonging to the early Mi'kmaq (also spelled Micmac) tribe in Nova Scotia bear striking comparisons to those of ancient Egypt, it seems certain that not all Native American ancestors migrated from Asia. A sampling of these, as previously published in *Beyond Any Shadow of Doubt*, by Niven Sinclair, is found in the Appendix, at the conclusion of this book.

The belief in six literal days of creation, the stories of the Garden of Eden, the two trees, and the initial sin, continue to spark controversy from all sides. It is most difficult to discern, in biblical drama, what is meant to be literal and what is meant to be allegorical. It seems very likely that the forbidden fruit was symbolic, denoting man's rebellion against divine authority. Regardless, the results are the same.

In keeping, it is important to note that the names of the biblical first couple, are themselves, words of symbolism. Adam (Hebrew אָדָם *Āḏām*) means man or mankind, while Eve (Hebrew הִוָּה *Ḥawwā*) means "living thing".

The man is referred to as *ha-āḏām* throughout the Genesis account, which may properly be translated as "earthling". As such, this does not indicate a proper name. The Bible says that "Adam called his wife's name Eve, because she was the mother of all living". [10]

Most ministers of the Christian faith choose to ignore the question of Cain's wife, or at the very least, avoid it in their teaching. It is now more commonly accepted by biblical scholars that Cain married one of his sisters, as borne out in the ***Book of Jubilees***. Evidently, this teaching was the belief of the ancient Jews.

We have no record to indicate how many children the biblical Adam and Eve were to have produced, but the Genesis account states that Adam "begot sons and daughters".[11] Life expectancy was reported to have been hundreds of years.

The Apocryphal ***Book of Jasher*** begins with the creation of Adam and Eve, completely omitting the biblical seven-day narrative. Following their expulsion from the garden, but before the story of the murder of Abel by Cain, the text states that the first couple had engendered two sons and three daughters.[12]

Assuming a literal Cain, marriage to a sister would not have been uncommon at this time. Even the patriarch, Abraham, married his own half-sister, Sarai, whose name was changed to Sarah. The Hebrew law against marriage to siblings was not given until the time of Moses. As alluded to earlier, the real quest for truth goes much deeper.

In further examining this subject, I want to use another verse from the first chapter of the Book of Genesis, or "beginnings".

After the initial creation story, in which no name is mentioned for the man or woman, it is recorded that YHWH said to the human couple, "Be fruitful and multiply, and replenish (Hebrew, *ûmil'û*) the earth, and subdue it…"[13] The word "replenish", according to the *Miriam-Webster Dictionary*, means "to fill with persons or animals; or to build up again". Clearly, this is in line with the original Hebrew used in this verse. Its specific meaning in this context, of course, continues to be greatly debated.

Was there a previous supply of earthlings before this *first* family? Were the names Adam and Eve allegorical to represent mankind which was placed on earth by divine design, perhaps the ancestral line of Israel? Scientific evidence, as I shall show, points to the fact that there were earthlings before our species.

Can evolution, to any extent, coexist with the biblical doctrine that man was created by God? Are science and the Bible to always exist at desperate odds, or can one be justified by the other?

While creationism is traditionally viewed as myth by most scientists, an increasing number of both geologists and theologians are attempting to tie the Bible stories together with archaeological findings. I will return to this subject later in the chapter.

Nuwaubian cult group leader Dr. Malachi Z. York teaches that there were several "replenishings" of earth before the time of the biblical "Adam". In *People of the Sun Scroll, #147*, he states that the name Adam refers to a title as well as a tribe.

He presents a theory which states that pre-historic earth was three times its present size. According to York, the ancient Egyptians were well aware of the existence of previous civilizations.[14]

Born Dwight D. York, he makes the fantastic claim of having come to earth from another galaxy, merely taking the body of Dwight York. This so-called walk-in, in addition to questionable credentials which include brushes with the law, bring York's theories under extreme scrutiny,[15] and yet, a teacher of Islamic Hebrew and Egyptology, he is the author of 460 books.[16]

In light of new evidence, it seems certain that there *were* previous civilizations, possibly explaining the existence of the Neanderthals. Recent DNA testing of a rib bone specimen, from an infant discovered in Southern Russia, dated 29,000 years old, shows that Neanderthals are *not* our direct ancestors, as previously thought.[17]

The species known as "Cro-Magnon", however, was fully human, and has now also been discovered in the Middle East. Might it be possible that the first biblical family was of this ilk? Scientific studies have dated these early humans at having lived 35,000 to 10, 000 years ago, taking them to the last ice age, overlapping the era of Neanderthals.[18]

Leonard W. King, Assistant Keeper of Egyptian and Assyrian Antiquities in the British Museum, and Professor at the University of London, King's College, published a book in 1916. Part of the "Schweich Lectures", it was titled *Legends of Babylon and Egypt in Relation to Hebrew Traditions*. He concluded that Babylonian texts, found in Nippur, which had been recently published at that time, written toward the end of the third millennium BC "incorporate traditions which extend in unbroken outline from their own period into the remote ages of the past, and claim to trace the history of man back to his creation. They represent the early national traditions of the Sumerian people, who preceded the Semites as the ruling race in Babylonia; and incidentally they necessitate a revision of current views with regard to the cradle of Babylonian civilization. The most remarkable of the new documents is one which relates in poetical narrative an account of the Creation, of Antediluvian history, and of the Deluge. It thus exhibits a close resemblance in structure to the corresponding Hebrew traditions, a resemblance that is not shared by the Semitic-Babylonian Versions at present known."[19]

It was in Lecture One that King quoted from the late Canon Driver, a gentleman who had delivered an earlier lecture (1908) in the Schweich series.

According to Driver, "The Babylonian narratives are both polytheistic, while the corresponding biblical narratives (Gen. i and vi-xi) are made the vehicle of a pure and exalted monotheism. In spite of this fundamental difference, as well as variations in detail, the resemblances are such as to leave no doubt that the Hebrew cosmogony and the Hebrew story of the Deluge are both derived ultimately from the same original as the Babylonian narratives, only transformed by the magic touch of Israel's religion, and infused by it with a new spirit."[20]

Today, members of the global scientific community are very familiar with these texts.

While sharing a common geocentric framework, the Sumerian and Babylonian creation legends differ sharply from those in Egypt. Some similarities to the biblical stories, however, are worthy of note.

In the oldest Sumerian myths, the minor gods, Emesh (summer), and his brother Enten (winter) had their individual parts in creation. Much in the way that Cain grew crops, and Abel tended flocks, Enlil produced trees, and was a builder, while Emesh was in charge of aiding sheep, goats, and other species such as birds and fish, in the process of giving birth and laying eggs.

A dispute arose between the god Enki and a mother goddess, Ninhursag, when Enki ate the plants which she had grown. Enraged, Ninhursag pronounced a curse of death on Enki. Eight parts of his body became diseased, one for each of the plants which he had eaten, one of which was his rib.

At first she disappeared, showing no sympathy, but eventually she relented, returning to heal Enki. She created eight healing goddesses, one for each of Enki's diseased parts. The goddess who healed his rib was called Nin-ti, which means, "lady of the rib". Students of Sumerian religion relate her to Eve.[21]

Allusions to the Heliopolitan creation myth, the most common of the four perpetuated in ancient Egypt, have survived the passage of the eras in several sources. *The Old Kingdom Pyramid Texts* and the *Coffin Texts* (the Middle Kingdom), *The Book of the Dead* (New Kingdom) and *Papyrus Bremner-Rhind*, all testify to this popular legend.[22]

Referring to Nu or Nun, this creation myth describes the churning sea of chaos that existed before creation. Out of this chaos arose the Egyptian sun god, Ra,[23] referred to as Atum Ra, or simply, Atum. Does this not sound alarmingly similar to the name of the first biblical man, Adam?

Although Atum was proclaimed to be self-created, his emergence from the primitive ocean might well remind us of the belief in the seas being able to form life by the rays of the sun. Atum, then, is said to have produced the "divine pair", Shu (air) and Tefnut (moisture). Might this equate to the biblical second day division of firmament and waters?

Shu and Tefnut became the parents of Geb (earth) and Nut (sky), who were, in turn, the parents of the four primary gods: Osiris and his wife Isis, Seth and his wife, in these legends, Nephthys. This system of nine gods, "The Ennead" became the predominant view, and was centered in Heliopolis [biblical "On"; Greek "Heliopolois", just north of modern Cairo].[24]

The origin of Seth in this creation story, which has similarities to the biblical narrative, would seem to indicate that the Egyptian god Seth and the biblical son of Adam might have had the same origin. This viewpoint is also shared by Professor Hugh Montgomery, author of the God-king series. In a recent personal email, Montgomery disclosed that this idea will be presented in his upcoming book, *The God-Kings of Outremer*.

The *Zohar*, a commentary on the Torah, is considered the most important work of Jewish mysticism. The existence of previous worlds, believed by some ancient Jews, was greatly debated. In the analysis of Genesis 1:2, the text states: "There are those who say that the Holy One created worlds and then destroyed them. Why were they destroyed? Because, as the Scripture says, 'the earth was tohu and bohu,' indicating the state of former worlds before their destruction. But would it not have been better if he had not created them? Most certainly it would, and the explanation involves a great mystery."[25]

Tohu and bohu are translated in the KJV Bible as "without form and void". Scholars have long debated the meaning of this verse, many believing that the ancient Jews were aware of a pre-adamic earth. The kabbalistic Jews of the early centuries felt that previous worlds had existed, and that the earth was a new creation. Tohu and bohu might easily relate to the chaos from which Egyptian myth claims Atum came forth.

The *Zohar* goes on to say: "The fact is, that the Holy One created the world and its population through the law expressed esoterically in the word 'brashith,' and referred to in the following passage: 'The Lord possessed me in the beginning of his way, and before he had created anything I was with him' (Prov. viii. 22); and by this brashith (beginning) he created the heavens and the earth, the foundations of which were based on 'berith' (law or covenant), the letters of which are contained in br(ash)ith. [*Hebrew for Genesis, my note*]

"It is of this berith that scripture speaks: 'If the law (or covenant) I have made had not existed, there would have been no day nor night, heaven nor earth' (Jer. xxxiii. 25), and it is of this law that scripture further states: 'The heavens are the Lord's, and he has given the earth to the children of men' (Ps. cxv. 16.).

"By the earth the Psalmist means our earth or world, which is one of seven worlds or earths referred to by David: 'I will walk before the Lord in the lands or earths of the living' (Ps. cxvi. 9). If, therefore, the Lord created worlds and destroyed them by reducing them to a state of tohu and bohu before the creation of the heavens and the earth, it was because the berith, or law, of such creation was not yet elaborated or existent. This is why the earth has escaped the fate of previous worlds."[26]

Modern DNA evidence indicates that our race first lived in Northeast Africa, in close proximity to ancient Egypt. The drama of the Garden of Eden is placed in Mesopotamia, where the ancient Sumerian and Babylonian legends originated. It needs to be shared, herein, that these locales are not far removed from the scientific origin of our species.

Evidence from archaeology and DNA also demonstrates that this planet has existed for a significantly longer time span that previously thought. In keeping with all life therein, this appears to be drastically out of agreement with the generations of Adam's descendants as listed in the scriptures. In accordance with the genealogical recordings in the Bible, comparing one chart to another, it is more than obvious that some generations have been omitted.

Much of the new trend toward creationism in the scientific community started in the 1960s, when scientists began to notice a connection between a number of previously unexplained coincidences in physics. They discovered that many mysterious relationships could be explained by the overriding fact that such values had been necessary for the creation of life. Robert Dicke was the first physicist to draw attention to this, followed by the interest of John Wheeler, a most prestigious practitioner of cosmetology.

In the fall of 1973, a conference in Poland was attended by the world's most eminent astronomers and physicists. Of all of the presented lectures, only the one delivered by prominent astrophysicist and cosmetologist Brandon Carter of Cambridge University would be remembered for decades to come.

His subject was "Large Number Coincidences and the Anthropic Principle in Cosmetology" (anthropic is Greek indicating "pertaining to mankind"). The anthropic principle states in plain English, "all of the seemingly arbitrary and unrelated constants in physics have one thing in common – these are precisely the values you need if you want to have a universe capable of producing life".

According to an article by Phillip Glynn, published in 1997 by Prima Publishing, this principle "raised fundamental questions about the modern interpretation of Copernicanism, but ultimately about Darwinism as well. It certainly showed that Darwin's theory of 'natural selection' could no longer be taken as an exhaustive explanation for the phenomenon of life."[27]

Although the vast majority of scientists reject the 6,000 year old earth theory, when it comes to "creation", a slightly different picture appears to be emerging. A recent survey of American scientists showed that about 40% believe in a personal God, and thus, likely about the same percentage believe in some form of creation, whether it be theistic evolution, progressive creation, the gap theory (an undetermined time lapse between Genesis 1:1 and verse 2), or young-earth creationism.[28]

Emblazoned upon the opposite side of the *divine design* coin are some more liberal theologians who feel that evolution was involved in "God's way of creating", and is not inconsistent with Christian faith. Among these is George L. Murphy of St. Mark Lutheran Church in Tallmadge, Ohio. His thoughts on the subject are explained in a detailed article, "A Theological Argument for Evolution", found at his web site.[29]

A fascinating book by Rabbi Moshe Shlomo Emanuel, entitled **Divine Design** draws from such writings as those of Sha'afel Aharon in **Shemot**, and the **Book (sefer) of Adam Harishon** concerning Betzalel, the son of Uri, a master craftsman of the tribe of Yehudah (Judah) [chief architect of the Tabernacle] who, mentioned twice in the Torah, was granted *secret wisdom* by Hashem (God, Judean Hebrew).

According to Rabbi Emanuel, a true understanding of his name and its meaning meant that the secrets of creation, the universe, and Judaism could be revealed. He also states that the process involved in God's creation of the world, after "consulting with the Torah" can be understood with an allegory.[30]

In examining all of the evidence, there are several factors which appear to point toward a single origin and destiny of modern man at some distant and undeterminable point in mystical pre-history.

These include:

1) Current DNA evidence that demonstrates, without a doubt, that all of mankind came from a single source in Northeast Africa.

2) Current DNA testing which indicates that our species did not descend from the extinct Neanderthals, though a possible inner-mixing with them may have occurred.

3) The higher intelligence, reasoning level, and sense of moral judgment attributed to mankind that greatly transcends the most advanced forms of lower animal life, seemingly indicating a special purpose of divine design.

4) The fact that ancient man believed in the divine, as has been evidenced by the creation stories that have prevailed within their societies.

The game of Chinese whispers, also known as the telephone game or grapevine, which I learned as a child, probably best explains the various versions of the creation story, and why they often contain similar characters and themes.

Each participant whispers a "secret" to the next in a line, and by the time it reaches the final player, many distortions have occurred. As the ancients passed down the tales of their common ancestors, the original version often became vastly misinterpreted, as have surnames over the past few centuries. My own family name reportedly has over one hundred spellings, a fact which merely serves to strengthen the belief in the common forebears whom we all share.

This subject of creationism is further expanded in chapters two and six.

Chapter 1 Footnotes

[1]Genesis 2:21-24
[2]Genesis 4:8
[3]Genesis 4:16
[4]Genesis 4:17
[5]*The Book of Jubilees*, IV.9
Retrieved February 2008 from The Internet Sacred
Text Archive located at
http://ftp.fortunaty.net/com/sacred-
texts/bib/jub/jub16.htm
[6]*The Book of Jubilees*, IV.11
Retrieved February 2008 from The Internet Sacred
Text Archive located at
http://ftp.fortunaty.net/com/sacred-
texts/bib/jub/jub16.htm
[7]Kraentzler, Ernst-Friedrich. (1978).
Ancestry of Richard Plantagenet & Cecile de
Neville: A royal study and charting to the beginning
(chart 1844, p 402). Automated Printing Systems,
Inc.: Salt Lake City, UT.
[8]Pope, John A. (Ed.) (1994). Cain. *Who's Who in*
the Bible (p 62). Readers Digest Association:
Pleasantville, NY.
[9]Ritter, Malcolm. (2008). *Indian DNA Links to 6*
'Founding Mothers'.
Retrieved February 2008 from
Yahoo News at
http://news.yahoo.com/s/ap/20080313/ap_on_sc/nat
ive_american_dna
[10]Genesis 3:20
[11]Genesis 5:4

[12]Jasher 1:12
Retrieved February 2008 from The Internet Sacred
Text Archive located at
http://www.sacred-texts.com/chr/apo/jasher/1.htm
[13]Genesis 1:28b
[14]York, Dr. Malichi Z. *The Replenishings of Earth:
Extracted from People of the Sun Scroll #147.*
Retrieved February 2008 from
http://www.nuwaubian-
hotep.net/docs/replenishings_of_earth.html
[15]*Dwight York.* Retrieved February 2008 from
Wikipedia, the free encyclopedia website located at
http://en.wikipedia.org/wiki/Dwight_York
[16]*The Master Teacher, Dr. Malachi Z. York.*
Retrieved February 2008 from
http://www.geocities.com/Area51/Corridor/4978/
york.html
[17]Siteclopedia Network. (2007). *Evolution Channel:
Neandertal Milestones.* Retrieved February 2008
from http://www.brainchannels.com/evolution/
neandertal.html
[18]About.com. (2008). *Archaeology: Cro-Magnon.*
Retrieved February 2008 from
http://archaeology.about.com/od/cterms/g/
cromagnon.htm
[19]King, Leonard W. (1916). *Legends of Babylonia
and Egypt.* "Lecture One : Egypt, Babylon and
Palestine, and Some Traditional Origins of
Civilization". Retrieved February 2008
From http://www.sacred-texts.com/ane/beheb.htm

[20]King, Leonard W. (1916). *Legends of Babylonia and Egypt*. "Lecture One : Egypt, Babylon and Palestine, and Some Traditional Origins of Civilization". Retrieved February 2008 from http://www.sacred-texts.com/ane/beheb.htm
[21]Crystal, Ellie. (2008). *Sumerian Gods and Goddesses*. Retrieved February 2008 from http://www.crystalinks.com/sumergods.html
[22]Rocheleau, Caroline. *Ancient Egypt Creation Myths*. Retrieved February 2008 from http://www.egyptvoyager.com/religionlessons_3_part1.htm
[23]All About History.org. (2008). *Egyptian Gods-Universal Truth*. Retrieved February 2008 from http://www.allabouthistory.org/egyptian-gods.htm
[24]Smith, William Stevenson. (1998). *The Art and Agriculture of Ancient Egypt* (p 5). Yale University Press: New Haven, CT.
[25]Hare, John Bruno. (2007). *Zohar:Genesis:Chapter VII, Previous Worlds and Races*.
Retrieved February 2008 from The Internet Sacred Text Archive located at http://www.sacred-texts.com/jud/zdm/zdm017.htm
[26]Ibid.
[27]Glynn, Patrick. (1997). *God: The Evidence* (pp 73-74). Prima Publishers: New York, NY.
[28]All About Creation.org. (2008). *Evidence for Creation*. Retrieved February 2008 from http://www.allaboutcreation.org/evidence-for-creation-faq.htm

[29]Murphy, George L. *A Theological Argument for Evolution*. Retrieved February 2008 from American Scientific Affiliation located at http://www.allaboutcreation.org/evidence-for-creation-faq.htm

[30]Emanue, Rabbi Moshe Shlomo. (2006). *Divine Design* (pp 22-24). Targum Press: Southfield, MI.

Adam and Eve in the Garden
by Albrecht Durer

Chapter Two
The Sons of God
Who Married the Daughters of Men
Before the Flood

The pre-flood era, also called the antediluvian age, is perhaps the most controversial and mystifying time frame in biblical pre-history. The following scripture verses from Genesis have also raised no small controversy. There are several very distinctive interpretations of their meaning which are commonly recognized.

"And it came to pass, when men began to multiply on the face of the earth, and daughters were born unto them, That the sons of God saw the daughters of men that they *were* fair; and they took them wives of all which they chose."[1] Shortly afterward, this thread continues: "There were giants in the earth in those days; and also after that, when the sons of God came in unto the daughters of men, and they bear *children* to them, the same *became* mighty men which were of old, men of renown."[2]

Immediately after this, the wickedness, or evil state of mankind, causes God to plan the destruction of them through the Great Deluge, also known as the flood of Noah's day.

Popular Christian teaching tells us that the "sons of God" in this text are those of the "godly line of Seth", Adam's third son, because they bore the character of the Creator God, whereas the daughters of men were of the other descendants of Adam and

Eve. Interestingly enough, there was an Egyptian god, mentioned in chapter one, by the name of Seth. The cognomen Meryet-Nit, one claimed Egyptian label for Seth's wife, sometimes spelled Mer-Neith, is also thought to have been the mother of king Den, and thus the wife of king Djet, third ruler of the First Dynasty of Egypt.[3]

Could Djet have been another form of Set, or Seth? The biblical Seth was the third son of Adam. Might he have been the equivalent of the Egyptian "god"? It is here that the reader may wish to also refer to chapters one and five for additional information.

Arguments for the "godly line of Seth" doctrine (a phrase *not* found in the Bible) state that the Hebrew word "elohim" (אלהים), is used to depict the human leaders in the twenty-first chapter of the Book of Exodus[4], there translated "judges", and in the eighty-second Psalm[5], translated "gods". This verse reads, "God standeth in the congregation of the mighty, and judgeth among the gods".

Is it possible that this scripture might be referring to the very human leaders who had been deemed gods? Dr. Edward Hindson, of Liberty University, founded by the late Dr. Jerry Falwell, is of this belief. He makes mention in his Liberty Bible Commentary that "archeology attests to the fact that a Near Eastern King would consistently be referred to as the son of his god".[6]

It would have also been likewise for both the Chinese and Roman Emperors. Norse rulers considered themselves the descendants of Odin, whom they viewed as a god.

Part of verse six of Psalm eighty-two was quoted by Jesus in the Gospel of John, chapter ten[7], to the unbelieving Jews, of his claim that he was the son of God. The entire verse reads, "I have said ye are gods (elohim); and all of you children of the Most High."

A belief belonging to the Church of Jesus Christ of Latter Day Saints, as brought out in the ***Book of Abraham***, teaches a pre-birth existence of humanity. Here they are called "the spirit children of the Eternal Father", and "the intelligences that were organized before the world was."[8]

Recently, Timberly Whitfield of *New Morning*, a Hallmark Channel TV program produced by Faith Streams, made a profound quote when she said that "We are not human beings having a spiritual experience, we are spiritual beings having a human experience." I was later to learn that these words belonged to internationally renowned author Dr. Wayne W. Dyer, affectionately called "the father of motivation".

Some believe that these "sons of God" were a separate creation of man, as described in chapter one. Others have gone so far as to suggest that these pre-historic giants were the offspring of humans having mated with animals. Another prominent view is that these "sons of God" were fallen angels, or spirit beings. This theory attempts to explain the reason for the fatal wickedness of mankind which causes God to destroy his own creation.

The Hebrew word in Genesis six, translated in the King James Bible as "giants", is נפילם, pronounced Nephilim, the plural of nephel, literally meaning rejects[9], or throw outs, so to speak. Both the New American Bible and the NIV use the word Nephilim, rather than attempt to translate.

A common belief among biblical scholars is that one third of the angels, or supernatural messengers of Yahweh, were cast from heaven, resulting from the rebellion of Lucifer. While there is no biblical text which states this, Revelation 12 has often been cited. This is where John the Revelator wrote that he saw "a great red dragon...and his tail drew the third part of the stars of heaven and did cast them to the earth".[10] Whether or not the "one-third" theory is a valid teaching, the doctrine of fallen angels was commonly believed in ancient days.

The Jewish prophet Isaiah described the rebellion of Lucifer, the "Angel of Light", against Yahweh in chapter fourteen of the book bearing his name[11], and stated that he was "fallen from heaven".

The Book of Job, as I shall bring out in the next chapter of this book, described a meeting of Lucifer, therein called "Satan", with Yahweh, in which he is quoted as saying that he had been "going to and fro in the earth, and walking up and down in it."[12]

The belief and teaching that Nephilim were the offspring of angels is supported in two ancient non-canonical writings of ancient Israel; namely, the **Book of Enoch** and the **Book of Jubilees**:

From the **Book of Enoch,** chapter three:

3.6.1 And it came to pass when the children of men had multiplied that in those days were born unto them beautiful and comely daughters. 2 And the angels, the children of the heaven, saw and lusted after them, and said to one another: 'Come, let us choose us wives from among the children of men 3 and beget us children.' And Semjaza, who was their leader, said unto them: 'I fear ye will not 4 indeed agree to do this deed, and I alone shall have to pay the penalty of a great sin.' And they all answered him and said: 'Let us all swear an oath, and all bind ourselves by mutual imprecations 5 not to abandon this plan but to do this thing.' Then sware they all together and bound themselves 6 by mutual imprecations upon it. And they were in all two hundred; who descended in the days of Jared on the summit of Mount Hermon, and they called it Mount Hermon, because they had sworn 7 and bound themselves by mutual imprecations upon it. And these are the names of their leaders: Samiaza, their leader, Araklba, Rameel, Kokablel, Tamlel, Ramlel, Danel, Ezeqeel, Baraqijal, 8 Asael, Armaros, Batarel, Ananel, Zaq1el, Samsapeel, Satarel, Turel, Jomjael, Sariel. These are their chiefs of tens.

From the *Book of Enoch*, chapter seven:

1 **And all the others together with them took unto themselves wives, and each chose for himself one, and they began to go in unto them and to defile themselves with them**, and they taught them charms 2 and enchantments, and the cutting of roots, and made them acquainted with plants. **And they** 3 **became pregnant, and they bare great giants,** whose height was three thousand ells: Who consumed 4 all the acquisitions of men. And when men could no longer sustain them, the giants turned against 5 them and devoured mankind. And they began to sin against birds, and beasts, and reptiles, and 6 fish, and to devour one another's flesh, and drink the blood. Then the earth laid accusation against the lawless ones.

From the *Book of Jubilees*, chapter five:

1 And it came to pass when the children of men began to multiply on the face of the earth and daughters were born unto them, that the angels of God saw them on a certain year of this jubilee, that they were beautiful to look upon; and they took themselves wives of all whom they chose, and **they bare unto them sons and they were giants**. 2 And lawlessness increased on the earth and all flesh corrupted its way, alike men and cattle and beasts and birds and everything that walks on the earth, all of them corrupted their ways and their orders, and they began to devour each other, and lawlessness increased on the earth and every imagination of the thoughts of all men (was) thus evil continually.

3 And God looked upon the earth, and behold it was corrupt, and all flesh had corrupted its orders, and all that were upon the earth had wrought all manner of evil before His eyes. 4 And He said that He would destroy man and all flesh upon the face of the earth 5 which He had created. But Noah found grace before the eyes of the Lord.

Let us now take a closer look at the evidence.

Much of the wording from these non-canonical writings parallels the Genesis account. If these words are taken as fact, then it could be more readily explained why God chose to bring a flood to destroy this "evil generation".

The term "sons of God" ("bene elohim" or slight variations) is found only five times in the Old Testament. Genesis six has already been covered. In the Book of Job, the term "sons of God" are mentioned three times.

Job, chapter one, verse six reads: "Now there was a day when the sons of God came to present themselves before the Lord, and Satan came also among them." Traditional Christians have no trouble with this relating to angels, readily admitting that Satan (the same as Semjaza?) was the leader of the fallen angels. This seems to indicate that fallen angels, according to the canon scripture, still had access to "the throne of God".

The first verse of the second chapter of Job is a later repeat of the presentation of the angelic beings before God. In Job thirty-eight, verses four and seven, the writer of the book says: "4 Where wast thou when I laid the foundations of the earth...7 When the morning stars sang out together, and all the sons of God shouted for joy?"

It is indisputable that the passages in Job refer to angels.

The other scripture is found in the third chapter of Daniel[13], ("bar elohim") and has reference to the "fourth man" in the fiery furnace, along with three Hebrews, at the order of Nebuchadnezzar, when they refused to worship him. It states that the personage was "like the Son of God". The author of Daniel calls him an angel.

Based on these particular writings, it seems most probable that the "sons of God" in Genesis 6 were angels, meaning non-human messengers from "heaven".

The Septuagint, the *Moffatt Translation of the Bible*, and some other versions, read: "angels of God", rather than "sons of God", as in Genesis 6.

Josephus taught this doctrine, for he stated, "**many angels of God accompanied with women, and begat sons that proved unjust, and despisers of**

all that was good, on account of the confidence they had in their own strength, for the tradition is that these men did what resembled the acts of those whom the Grecians call giants".[14]

With the discovery of the **Dead Sea Scrolls** in 1947, another source for historical evidence of the pre-deluge cohabitation of "angels" with women, thereby producing a race of giants, was to become available.

In addition to the **Book of Enoch**, already in common usage, seven fragments contained portions of the **Book of Giants**, previously known only through scattered allusions to it in Central Asian manuscripts.

This book retells part of the story from the **Book of Enoch**, further elaborating on the lives of some of the giants. It creates a picture of Enoch attempting to interpret a dream of judgment, interceding with God on behalf of the giants. Gilgamesh, the hero of the Babylonian flood epic, is noted as being one of the giants.

Sounding much like the Apocalypse, one fragment said "the Ruler of Heaven came down to earth".[15]

The text of the **Book of Giants** goes on to say, "and thrones were set out and the Great Holy One sa[t ...were] serving him a thousand thousands [...be]fore him were standing and behold [...] were opened and a judgment was uttered and judgment [...written and signed with a mark [...] all that lived and everything mortal and [...] that was the end of the dream. [thereupon] all the giants were afraid..." They are said to have consulted Enoch for the interpretation.[16]

In the second chapter of the New Testament epistle of II Peter, the scenario of the pre-flood earth is replayed. "If God spared not the **angels who sinned**, but cast them down to hell, and delivered *them* into chains of darkness, to be reserved unto judgment; And spared not the **old world**, but saved Noah the eighth *person*, a preacher of righteousness, bringing in the flood upon the world of the ungodly..." These verses go together as a common unit. If it were believed that the angels who sinned had nothing to do with the evil condition of the pre-flood world, then why is it mentioned here by the apostle Peter? In Jude 6, these are called "the angels that kept not their first estate, but left their own habitation".[17]

A strange thought here is that Dr. Hindson, who opposed the idea of the angels' marriage to women in his commentary on II Peter 2:4, now notes: "Compare Genesis 6:1-4".

In opposition to this theory, many quote Jesus in his parallel statements recorded in the Gospels of Matthew and Mark: "For in the resurrection they [the resurrected] neither marry, nor are given in marriage, but are as the angels of God in heaven."[18]

"For when they shall rise from the dead, they neither marry, nor are given in marriage; but are as the angels which are in heaven."[19]

Here Jesus was combating the doctrine of humans being married in the next life. Note exactly the way this is phrased: "neither marry, nor or given in marriage". It does not say that they are asexual beings, only that they do not marry in heaven.

All angels mentioned in scripture are given a male gender. If angels who were fallen from the heavenly realm were sexual beings, or due to their supernatural abilities chose to be so, is it not a possibility that they could be? In keeping, is it not a possibility that they could have sired offspring?

In the Gnostic *Book of Melchizedek*, a statement is made regarding "the achons and all the angels, together with the seed <which> flowed down from the Father of the All..." and a bit further down in the text, "For when they ate of the tree of knowledge, they trampled the Cherubim and the Seraphim with the flaming sword. They [   ] which was Adam's [   ] the world-rulers, and [   ] them out [   ] after they had brought forth [   ] offspring of the archons and their worldly things, these belonging to ..."(*13 lines unrecoverable)*[20]

According to the About.com web site "archon, in Greek, means 'authority', and comes from the same root as 'arch', as in 'archangel.'" According to Gnostic belief, "Archons were planetary rulers and guardians of the seven visible planets, and perceived as agents of the Demiurge, predatory beings who inhibit spiritual awakening by convincing humanity of a false reality; they are the forces of sin, fear, and temptation."[21] It is obvious that the writer, in keeping with other ancients, believed that the Nephilim were indeed the seed of the Archons.

In Islamic mythology, two angels, Harut and Marut, became masters of evil. A group of angels who were ridiculing man's wickedness were sent to earth.[22]

It seems clear from these numerous corresponding texts that the daughters of men being referred to are the female descendants of the Adamic seed, while the *sons of God are a totally separate race, notwithstanding belief in the spiritual nature of man.*

The fallen angels are also known as the "Watchers". Watchers first appeared in Sumer. "Shumer", an alternate spelling, reportedly meant, "Land of the Watchers".[23]

Present day UFO sightings have led to the inference, by some authors, that these Watchers were beings from another planet, perhaps even another galaxy.

A pioneer in the theory of ancient alien visitation was Erich von Daniken, whose 1968 book, ***Chariots of the Gods***, first translated into English in 1969, caused a flurry of denial and controversy among students and proponents of the Bible.

A subsequent television special, *In Search of Ancient Astronauts*, broadened the controversy. Additional books by von Daniken and others, have continued to present striking evidence that space travel may well have occurred in ancient times.

According to a report aired on the NBC's *Today Show* on February 23, 2008, almost half of all Americans believe that we have been visited by aliens from outer space.

Both the shrouded secrecy of the Roswell, New Mexico incident in 1947 and the long-term denial of the existence of Nevada's Area 51, as perpetuated by the American government, has only added fuel to the numerous conspiracy theories concerning extraterrestrial visitations.[24] If, indeed, these extraterrestrials exist, who are they?

Simply having been exposed to a doctrine by a specific group, as most have, does not make it true.

Are we to simply accept without examination? I think not.

Chapter 2 Footnotes

[1]Genesis 6:1 and 2

[2]Genesis 6:4

[3]*Egyptian Kings: Meryet Neit* website.
Retrieved February 2008 from
http://www.nemo.nu/ibisportal/0egyptintro/2egypt/2
sidor/2mery.htm

[4]Exodus 21:6

[5]Psalm 82:1

[6]Hindson, Edward E. (1963). *Liberty Bible Commentary* (p 1086). Thomas Nelson Publishers: Camden, NY.

[8] Abraham 3:19-24.

[9]*Bibleprobe* website. Retrieved February 2008 from http://www.bibleprobe.com/nephilim.htm

[10]Revelation 12:2-3

[11]Isaiah 14:12-15

[12]Job 1:6-12

[13]Daniel 3:25-28

[14]Wiston, William. (1987). *The Works of Josephus, Complete and Unabridged* (p 32). Hendrickson Publishers: Peabody, MA as taken from Flavius Josephus, *Antiquities of the Jews*, Book 1.3.1 (73).

[15]Wise, Michael, Aregg Jr, Martin and Cook, Edward. (2005). *The Dead Sea Scrolls, A New Translation* (p 290). Harper San Francisco: New York, NY.

[16] Ibid.

[17]II Peter 2:4-5

[18]Matthew 22:30

[19]Mark 12:25

[20] *The Nag Hammadi Library*. Retrieved February 2008 from Gnostic *Society Library* website located at http://www.webcom.com/~gnosis/naghamm/melchiz.html

[21] About.com. (2008). *Archons*. Retrieved February 2008 from http://altreligion.about.com/library/glossary/bldefarchons.htm

[22] Coppens, Philip. (1996). *The rise of the Watchers*. Retrieved February 2008 from http://www.philipcoppens.com/watchers.html

[23] Ibid.

[24] About.com. (2008). *Area 51: Top Secret Government Facility*. Retrieved February 2008 from http://ufos.about.com/od/governmentconspiracyufos/p/area51.htm

**Sons of God
Marry Daughters of Men
by Das Buch der Büücher in Bilden**

Chapter Three
Job

One of the most elusive characters portrayed in the canonic scriptures is known to most as "Job" (Hebrew, **איוב** , Arabic ابوي).

This highly discussed and often disagreed upon writing is seen as one of the oldest[1] books in the world. It is, almost certainly, the most ancient work found in Hebrew texts. Some conclude that this story, like many antiquated tales, was passed down verbally from generation to generation, not formally penned until the time of David and Solomon (1000-922 BC). Others believe that its writing occurred around the time of King Hezekiah (715-687 BC), suggesting that the poetic form of the book was composed during the Babylonian exile.[2] The Hebrew language of the narrative, however, is that of the Patriarchal Period, blended with both Syriac and Arabic. Consequently, it is my feeling that its first writing most likely occurred early in the history of Mesopotamian literature. In addition, Job contains more rare words than any other book in the Bible, and all scholars agree on the complexity of the dialogue.[3]

The meaning of his name in Hebrew is uncertain. Some possibilities include "where is the Father (God)", and "an enemy/persecuted one". In Arabic, the name is pronounced Ayyūb or Iyyov, and is thought to be derived[4] from the word "tawbah", often translated, "repentance", which literally means "to return". [5]

In Christendom, Job has become the symbolic personification of patience. His character was a personage of great endurance and integrity. In the biblical narrative, God is quoted as saying "there is none like him in the earth, a perfect and upright man..."[6]

After enduring every test imagined against him, the Bible states that he retained his faith in the God of heaven. It is also written that, in the end, his fortune and family became greater than that which was taken away.

But who was this fabled man of old? When and where is he most likely to have lived? What is the origin of this tale of woe and glory? Was he a Jew? The more questions that are posed, the more complex the answers seem to become.

Similar stories, like those of both the creation and the flood, have been told in many ancient Near Eastern works of literature dated prior to the second millennium BC. An Egyptian hieroglyphic document from the twenty-first century BC, called *The Protests of the Eloquent Peasant*, is made up of a similar series of speeches addressed to a pharaoh who was seen as a god.

The most controversial view of Job's personage is that he was indeed a pharaoh, himself, and none other than the builder of the Great Pyramid, Khufu. (c. 2551-2528 BC). He was also known as Cheops, with a silent s, which sounds very much like Job. This is the theory that was expressed by the late Herbert W. Armstrong, in the 1950's, founder of the Worldwide Church of God, in a booklet titled *Who Was Job?*

Armstrong saw references to laying the foundations of the world, and the wealth and fame of Job, coupled with Job's statement regarding his position and authority[7], to mean that he was a king who was involved in a great construction project.

There exists a Canaanite story of Keret, a man who, like Job, loses his wife and sons, but gains a new family after regaining the approval of the gods. In addition, there are at least four Mesopotamian texts which share common themes to Job, the closest being *Man and his God*, referred to by some scholars as "the Sumerian Job". These parallels merely serve to indicate that a story such as this was both well known and believed throughout the ancient Eastern nations.

The biblical Job, nonetheless, seems certain to declare a vivid portrayal of a specific sage of old. Some verbiage concerning him may have indeed been derived from earlier texts. There are specific factors that must be considered in studying this character, before drawing a conclusion.

He is never identified as an Israelite. The time period in which his story takes place is most likely during what is known to scholars as the "late Patriarchal Period". In other words, sometime after the life of Abram, Hebrew: אַבְרָם, meaning "exalted father", later known as Abraham, אַבְרָהָם, meaning "father of many", patriarch of the Israelites and the Arabs. (See chapter eleven)

Job possibly lived in the early nineteenth century BC. There are several points of consideration that work toward presenting this particular conclusion. First, since Job's saga was included among the stories of the Israelites, it is likely to have had Hebrew/Semitic origins.

Josephus (37-100 AD), the most famous and respected of the Jewish historians not included in the scriptures, saw Heber or Eber[8] as the progenitor of the name "Hebrews". Heber, the grandson of Noah's son, Shem, was an ancestor of Abraham. According to the Book of Genesis[9], Abram had a brother named Nahor.

Josephus, in *Antiquities of the Jews,* stated that Nahor had eight sons by his wife, Milcha, as well as others by his concubine, Reuma. One of his sons was named Uz.[10]

Many of the cities and countries were given the name of the person who settled it, as later occurred with the land of Israel. A city of this area was named Nahor. Elihu, who started his evaluation of

Job in the thirty-second chapter, was the son of Barachel the Buzite. This most likely indicated that he was descended from Buz, a son of Nahor.

The biblical narrative begins, "there was a man in the land of Uz, whose name was Job".[11] Though there is much speculation about the land of Uz, it seems likely that it was the territory settled by the son of Nahor, and/or his descendants. Uz is believed to have been located in the area of Arabia and Edom, inhabited by the descendants of Esau.

The next factor to consider is the places of residence recorded for the three friends of Job. Esau, Jacob's twin brother, had a son named Eliphaz[12], who had a son named Teman.[13] Job's friend, Eliphaz was called a Temanite. He may have been named for his ancestor. Although Esau was a worshiper of Yahweh, as was his father Abraham, he broke from these teachings by marrying two Canaanite women, one of whom was Adah, mother of Eliphaz, meaning "God is my strength".

Baal worship was common among the Canaanites. Abraham is most commonly thought of as having only one wife, Sarah, who late in life gave birth to Isaac, and a concubine, Hagar, her handmaid, the mother of Ishmael. This story will be discussed in detail in a later chapter.

However, Abraham fathered several additional sons by his other wife, Keturah. These joined his exiled son, Ishmael, becoming part of the Arabic nation.

Keturrah's sons were Zimran, Joshan, Medan, Midian, Ishbak, and Shuah.[14]

Bildad the Shuhite, another of Job's friends, was almost certainly a descendant of Shuah. Since Abraham left all of his inheritance to Isaac[15], the other sons received no further mention in the Torah. The LXX, commonly known as the Septuagint, meaning the Greek rendering of the Hebrew Scriptures translated in Alexandria, Egypt in the third century BC, identifies Zophar the Naamathite as, a "king of the Mineans", or the Ma'in. The Maonites mentioned in the tenth chapter of the Book of Judges,[16] lived in Southern Arabia.[17]

Also, as an inhabitant of Uz, Job is very possibly one of Nahor's descendants, and most definitely a leader among his people. Job was a very eloquent speaker. An educated man, he possessed great wealth and influence. He had both man and maid servants. Clearly, this was a man who displayed great knowledge of the world of his day. He was also a man of staunch faith in one God, as evidenced in the lengthy recorded discourse, beginning in chapter twenty-five of the book which bears his name.[18]

Although not likely to have been a pharaoh, he is quoted as stating that he "sat as a chief, and dwelt as a king in the army".[19] Unto him "men gave ear, and waited, and kept silence at his counsel".[20]

He knew of the famed gold of Ophir, likely a seaport in southern Arabia, although there are some who believe that Ophir was located in modern Somaliland. Ophir was probably named for a son of Joktan[21], a grandson of Heber. The gold of Ophir is mentioned ten times in the Old Testament. Job also mentions silver and precious stones, of which he is obviously a possessor.

The line of Isaac's son, Esau, lived in the area between the Dead Sea and the Gulf of Aqabah.[22] Although they were enemies of Israel, the stories of their ancestor, Abraham, and his offspring, would certainly have been known by both Israelites and Arabs. In *the Qur'an*, Ayyub is listed among the prophets of Islam.[23] Many Muslims have expressed their views of this lineage which, albeit not in complete harmony, show at least two ascendant charts from Esau.[24]

Despite the fact that Job's early comments about the finality of death show very little knowledge of traditional Abrahamic religious teachings, a remarkable quotation from him in the nineteenth chapter[25] is seen as a messianic prophecy by both Jews and Christians alike, thereby serving to enforce the Islamic belief in Job as a prophet. It is here that he suddenly seems to be inspired with a vision of redemption, and an age of Heaven on Earth: "For I know my redeemer liveth, and *that* he shall stand at the latterday upon the earth".[26] The end of his statement forecasts a final judgment.

This time frame might also explain why it was stated that there was "none like" Job on the earth. It is known that by this time, the children of Israel had shown their ungodliness by selling Joseph into slavery, and according to many scholars, were already in Egypt, as Joseph's death most likely occurred about 1805 BC.

David J. Gibson, the author of **Whence Came the Hyksos Kings of Egypt**,[27] promotes the theory that Job was short for "Jobab", who was the second king of Edom according to the Book of Genesis.[28] This is both an interesting and logical conclusion. The true identity of the Hyksos kings, though not likely to include Job, is an important key to unlocking other mysteries in scripture. I will expound upon this in chapter five.

This theory was first put forth in the index of the **Septuagint**.[29] Even though Christian theologian James B. Jordan, of Biblical Horizons, describes their aim as "thoroughly Biblical, comprehensively catholic, and true to the Reformation faith", he firmly believes that Job was an Edomite king .[30]

Job's unfailing faith during adversity, as well as the ultimate blessing which he is recorded to have received, will always be a leading example to all proponents of the Abrahamic faiths.

Chapter 3 Footnotes

[1]Gospelcom.net (2008). *Jamieson-Faussett-Brown Bible Commentary*. Retrieved February 2008 from http://eword.gospelcom.net/comments/job/jfb/job1.htm

[2]*Repentance in Islam* retrieved from Wikipedia, the free encyclopedia website located at http://en.wikipedia.org/wiki/Repentance_in_Islam

[3]Job 1:8

[4] Poling, Daniel. (1956). *Your Questions Answered With Comforting Counsel* (p 38). Channel Press: Great Neck, NY.

[5]Pope, John A. (Ed.) (1994). Job. *Who's Who in the Bible* (p 228). Readers Digest Association: Pleasantville, NY.

[6]Poling, Daniel. (1956). *Your Questions Answered With Comforting Counsel* (p 38). Channel Press: Great Neck, NY.

[7]Job 29:25

[8]Genesis 11:16

[9]Genesis 11:24

[10]Wiston, William. (1987). *The Works of Josephus, Complete and Unabridged* (p 37). Hendrickson Publishers: Peabody, MA as taken from Flavius Josephus, *Antiquities of the Jews*, Book 1.6.5 (153).

[11]Job 1:1

[12]Genesis 36:4

[13]Genesis 36:11

[14]Genesis 25:1&2

[15] Genesis 25:5

[16]Judges 10:12

[17]Crossmap.com. (2008). *Zophar*. Retrieved
February 2008 from
http://dictionary.crossmap.com/definition/zophar.
htm
[18]Job 25:1-32:5
[19]Job 29:25
[20]Job 28:21
[21]Genesis10:29 and I Coronicles 1:23
[22]Alter, Robert. (204). *The Five Books of Moses:
A Tranlation with Commentary* (p 201).
William Norton & Co.: New York, NY.
[23]Ali, Ahmed. (1992). *The Sacred Writings of
Islam, The Qur'an* (p 280, ch 22, v 83). Book of the
Month Club: New York, NY.
[24]*Stories of The Prophets - Prophet Ayoub*.
Retrieved February 2008 from
http://anwary-islam.com/prophet-story/ayoub.htm
[25]Job 19: 23-29
[26]Job 19:25
[27]Gibson, David J. *The Hyksos, Kings of Egypt and
the land of Edom, Chapter IV, The Book of Job*.
Retrieved February 2008 from
http://nabataea.net/edomch4.html
[28]Genesis 36:33
[29] TheRain.org. (2008). The *Septuagint Ending of
the Book of Job*. Retrieved February 2008 from
http://www.therain.org/appendixes/app62.html
[30]Jordan, James B. (2000). *Was Job an Edomite
King?* Retrieved February 2008 from
http://www.biblicalhorizons.com/biblical-
horizons/no-131-was-job-an-edomite-king-part-2/

Chapter Four
Melchizedek

An even more mysterious and controversial individual in the Hebrew and Christian canon is Melchizedek, Hebrew: קֶדֶצ־יִכְּלְמַ. His name is first mentioned in the Book of Genesis[1], when he appears to Abram (about the twenty-second century BC), at a time of war in which Abram and his soldiers, 318 trained servants born in his household, had carried out the remarkable rescue of his nephew, Lot.

The Bible states that he was visited by two kings: first the unnamed king of Sodom, then the mysterious Melchizedek, King of Salem, meaning "peace". Josephus, in *Antiquities of the Jews*, says that Abram had adopted Lot.[2] This makes sense, based on his later concern of Sarai's barren state. He also makes note that the name Salem was later changed to Jerusalem.[3] From the writings of Flavius Josephus, it is obvious that he had access to ancient texts not included in the books of the *Tanakh*.

Statements about the personage of Melchizedek found in the Genesis texts are:

1) He was the king of Salem (peace).

2) He "brought forth bread and wine", the items which were later to become both emblems of the Passover as well as Eucharistic symbols of the Last Supper of Jesus Christ with the Apostles.

3) He was the "priest of the most high God (אל עליון El Elyon) possessor of heaven and earth".

4) He administered a blessing upon Abram and called him "of the most high God..."

5) He received tithes from Abram, the tenth which is most used to describe the portion of increase which were later decreed as belonging to God under Jewish law, apparently setting a precedent.

Hereafter, mention of Melchizedek is found no more in scripture until the messianic prophecy recorded in the Psalms[4]: "Thou art a priest for ever after the order of Melchizedek".

Reference to this illusive personage is found in the New Testament Epistle to the Hebrews, chapter seven. "For this Melchisedek, king of Salem, priest of the most high God, who met Abraham returning from the slaughter of the kings, and blessed him; To whom also Abraham gave a tenth part of all; first being by interpretation King of righteousness, and after that, King of Salem, which is **King of peace; Without father, without mother, without descent; having neither beginning of days, nor end of life; but made like unto the Son of God**; **abideth a priest continually.** Now consider how great this man was, unto whom even the patriarch Abraham gave the tenth of the spoils. And verily they that are the sons of Levi, who receive the office of this priesthood, have a commandment to take tithes of the people according to the law, that is of their brethren, though they came out of the loins of Abraham; But he whose descent is not counted from them received tithes of Abraham, and blessed him that he had the promises. And without all contradiction, the less is blessed of the better. And here **men that die** receive tithes; but there he receiveth them, of whom **it is witnessed that he liveth**". [5]

Based on the previous passage, we get a feeling that the writer of the Epistle to the Hebrews viewed Melchizedek as a *supernatural personage*. Not only was he said to be an eternal being, without parentage, beginning or end of life, *he also states that* **Melchizedek was greater than Abraham,** *the founder of the faith of the Jews.* He was called the King of righteousness, and, most notably, *"like unto the Son of God"*.

In the first verse of the very next chapter, Abraham had a vision of "the Lord", who spoke to him, promising that a son would spring forth from his own loins. Abraham was soon visited in person by "the Lord"[6] in the plains of Mamre in the heat of the day". The three in the company are also called "men". However, something made Abraham realize that these were not ordinary men, for he ran from his tent to meet them and "bowed himself toward the ground".[7] This is the famous incident in which scripture records that the promise of the vision was repeated in person to Abraham, that Sarah would conceive and bear Isaac. Ninety-year-old Sarah was so unbelieving that she is said to have laughed.

Three separate verses[8] begin, "And the Lord said...", indicating once again that one of his visitors was a deity. The passage[9] also indicates that the Lord would return after the child was born.

In addition, according to the Bible, the heavenly trio told Abraham of the fate which awaited Sodom and Gomorrah. Abraham thereby made an attempt to save the cities, the home of his dear nephew Lot. Chapter nineteen, verse one indicates that two angels, presumably the other two visitors, arrived in Sodom.

Chapter twenty-one, verse one says that the Lord visited Sarah. Immediately thereafter, she became pregnant with Isaac.

The identified scripture passages shared herein show that there appears to have been just cause to believe that Melchizedek was a deity, or certainly that Abraham perceived this to be so. Given this belief, there has been speculation by scholars that he was Yahweh, a "pre-incarnation" appearance of Jesus, or perhaps the angel, Michael.

In the ***Babylonian Talmud***, Jewish Rabbis identified Melchizedek with Shem, son of Noah.[10] The ***Zohar***, however, sees the meaning of "Melchizedek king of Salem" as "the King Who rules with complete sovereignty," or according to another explanation, that "Melchizedek" alludes to the lower world and "king of Salem" to the upper world.[11]

Not surprisingly, Melchizedek is also mentioned in the ***Dead Sea Scrolls***. Here he is seen by the author as the agent by whom debts are forgiven in the Year of Jubilee, the fiftieth year, following a succession of seven sabbatical years. One scroll contains five references to him. In part, it states, "...and whose teachers have been hidden and kept secr[et], even from the inheritance of Melchizedek, f[or ...] and they are the inherit[ance of Melchize]dek who will return to them what is rightfully theirs. He will proclaim to them the jubilee, thereby releasing th[em from the debt of a]ll their sins" In the next paragraph it calls the Year of Jubilee "the year of Melchiz[edek]'s favor".[12]

Commentator Dr. Edward E. Hindson states that he feels the deity of Melchizedek is unlikely[13], since the name Zedek is a dynastic title of Jebusite kings, as mentioned in the ***el-Amarna Letters***, tablets discovered some years ago at Tell el-Amarna in Egypt. These fascinating letters are the communication between the government of ancient Palestine and Niphururia, now thought to be Tutankhamon, Akhenaten or Smenkhare, the pharaoh of Egypt at the time of the Invasion of Palestine in the fourteenth century BC, by the Hebrews, called "Khabint"[14].

A king bearing the name Zedek is found in the Bible in the Book of Joshua.[15] Adoni-zedek, Hindson shares, was not a believer. So why did he have this name?

Adoni means "my lord". Zedek in West Semetic tongue means "Justice"[16], and was probably the chief god of the Jebusites. Melchizedek literally means "My king is Zedek", (justice, or righteousness, as expressed in the Book of Hebrews). It is possible, according to some students of ancient religion, that Zedek could have been the Jebusite name for Yahwah.

Since all are said to have descended from Noah only a few generations prior, could this not be true, no matter how misguided? Hindson speaks of Melchizedek having had an earthly kingdom at Salem. He says that Jesus was given a priesthood after the order of Melchizedek. If he were, would this not mean that the order was so named after himself? What if this meant that the order of the Messiah's priesthood was set up in symbolism in the Old Testament?

The theory that El Elyon (the most high god), whose priest was Melchizedek, was an ancient god of Salem, or Jerusalem, later equated with Yahweh, was first advanced by German biblical scholar Julius Wellhausen (1844-1918). According to Wellhausen, Zadokite priests of Jerusalem claimed to be descended from this Melchizedek, or at least to have inherited his position.[17]

The *Gnostic Book of Melchizedek* is mainly a praise of "Jesus Christ, the Son of God" from the second century AD. However, it also contains a statement, made in the first person, concerning

Melchizedek, indicating a being thought to be ever-existent. He is called "Holy One, High Priest, the perfect hope, and gifts of life".[18] In addition, he was viewed by some Gnostics to have been a previous incarnation of Jesus.

Who was Melchizedek? You decide.

Abraham Meets Melchizedek
Young People's Illustrated Bible **(1865)**

Chapter 4 Footnotes

[1]Genesis 14: 18
[2]Wiston, William. (1987). *The Works of Josephus, Complete and Unabridged* (p 38). Hendrickson Publishers: Peabody, MA as taken from Flavius Josephus, *Antiquities of the Jews*, Book 1.7.1 (154).
[3]Wiston, William. (1987). *The Works of Josephus, Complete and Unabridged* (p 39). Hendrickson Publishers: Peabody, MA as taken from Flavius Josephus, *Antiquities of the Jews*, Book 10.2 (180).
[4]Psalm 110:4
[5]Hebrews 7:1-8
[6]Genesis 18:1-16
[7]Ibid, verse 2
[8]Ibid, verses 13, 17, and 20
[9]Ibid, verse 14
[10]*Babylonian Talmud: Nedarim* 32b. Retrieved March 2008 from http://www.come-and-hear.com/nedarim/nedarim_32.html#PARTb
[11]Crystal, Ellie. (2008). *Melchizedek*. Retrieved February 2008 from http://www.crystalinks.com/melchizedek.html
[12]Wise, Michael, Aregg Jr, Martin and Cook, Edward. (2005). *The Dead Sea Scrolls, A New Translation* (p 290). Harper San Francisco: New York, NY.
[13]Hindson, Edward E. (196). *Liberty Bible Commentary* (p 255). Thomas Nelson Publishers: Camden, NY.
[14]Gibson, David J. *The Hyksos, Kings of Egypt and the land of Edom, Chapter VII, Religion and Date*

of the Edomite Empire. Retrieved February 2008 from
http://nabataea.net/edomch7.html
[15]Joshua 10:1
[16]*Zedek* retrieved from Wikipedia, the free encyclopedia website located at
http://en.wikipedia.org/wiki/Zedek
[17]*The Nag Hammadi Library*. Retrieved February 2008 from Gnostic *Society Library* website located at http://www.webcom.com/~gnosis/naghamm/melchiz.html
[18]*Elyon* retrieved from Wikipedia, the free encyclopedia website located at
http://en.wikipedia.org/wiki/Elyon

Chapter Five
Joseph and Israel in Egypt,
The Hyksos Kings, and
The Biblical Exodus

Similar to the curious absence in the New Testament of any mention of the Essenes, the biblical narratives in the *Torah* never mention the Hyksos Kings of the Fifteenth Dynasty in Egypt (c. 1675 to 1567 BC), or do they?

In the third century BC there was an historical record of the reign of the Hyksos Kings as recorded by Manetho, a Greco-Egyptian priest born at Sebennytos in the Nile Delta, who lived during the reign of Ptolemy I and Alexander the Great. He is thought to have been a priest of Atum Ra at Heliopolis, first mentioned in chapter one.

The writings of Manetho are of significant importance to the study of Egyptology because, in having provided such a detailed history of Egypt, such served to become the basic structure for the chronology of ancient Egypt, one still being used by historians today.[1]

Basing his story on unnamed "sacred books", and popular legends, Manetho described a massive brutal invasion by foreigners from the east whom he called Hyksos (Greek Ὑκσώς), which he translated as "shepherd kings", but in actuality, means "rulers of foreign lands".

He stated that these foreigners inhabited a delta city named Avaris (northeast of Memphis), now Tell ed-Daba. He further writes that they founded a dynasty which ruled with great cruelty for more than five hundred years,[2] a statement that now seems to have been a great exaggeration.

The names of some of the Hyksos kings were of West Semetic and/or Canaanite origin. Two examples, are Jacob-el (Ya' qub-'al), "May El give protection", and Jacob-baal, "May Baal protect".[3]

Although much of Manetho's original history is lost to us, Josephus claims to quote directly from his writings, the following words describing the claimed Hyksos invasion.

"There was a king of ours, whose name was Timaus. Under him it came to pass, I know not how, that God was averse to us; and there came, after a surprising manner, men of ignoble birth out of the eastern parts, and had boldness enough to make an expedition into our country, and with ease subdued us by force, yet without us hazarding a battle with them."[4]

Based on the previous name examples, either these foreigners were originally monotheistic, or they worshipped a supreme creator god, such as El (Baal), who was perceived as being capable of great wrath.

In speaking of them Manetho says, in essence, "God became angry with us", not "the gods", as in his later statement concerning the destruction of the temples of the Egyptian deities.

According to Christopher Knight and Robert Lomas in *The Hiram Key*, the Hyksos quickly started adopting Egyptian customs, taking as their state deity the god Set, or Seth, the brother of Osiris, similar in characteristics to the Canaanite god, Baal. They also honored Ra as a major god, building new temples, and idols. It has been claimed that the Hyksos also ruled the old capitol of Memphis for some time. Although the true Egyptian monarchy had lost that seat of control, they had been able to maintain their family presence, four hundred miles to the south of Avaris, in the city of Thebes.[5] As previously mentioned in chapter one, Ra was also known as Atum. These foreign kings acknowledged Atum (Adam) and Seth.

Of their capitol at Avaris, Josephus wrote, "Manetho says, 'The shepherds had built a wall around all this place, which was a large and strong wall, and this in order to keep all their possessions and their prey within a place of strength;'" [6]

Josephus immediately continues, "but that Thummosis, the son of Alisphragmuthosis, made an attempt to take them by force and by siege, with four hundred and eighty thousand men to lie around about them; but that, upon his despair of taking the place by that siege, they came to a composition with them that they should leave Egypt, and go, without any harm to be done them, wherever they would; and that after this composition was made they went away with their whole families and effects, not fewer in number than two hundred and forty thousand and took their journey from Egypt, through the wilderness, for Syria, but that as they were in fear of the Assyrians, who had then the dominion over Asia, they built a city in that country which is now called Judea and that large enough to contain this great number of men and called it Jerusalem." [7]

Here Josephus identifies the Hyksos as the Israelites themselves, for he states: "Now Manetho, in another book of his, says, 'That this nation, thus called Shepherds, was also called Captives, in their sacred books.' And this account of his is the truth; for feeding of sheep was the employment of our forefathers in the most ancient ages; and as they led such a wandering life in feeding sheep, they were called Shepherds. Nor was it without reason that they were called Captives by the Egyptians, since one of our ancestors, Joseph, told the king of Egypt that he was a captive, and afterwards sent for his brethren into Egypt by the king's permission; but as for these matters, I shall make a more exact inquiry about them elsewhere." [8]

In the further works of Josephus, no record is to be found in which he further explored this theory.

There are many varied theories, not only as to who these kings were, but how they might also align with the Israelite stay in Egypt.

What are the factors in favor of the Hyksos Israelite theory? Not only did the pharaohs have Semetic names, but they left Egypt and presumably built Jerusalem. If this is, indeed, the case, why is their time in Egypt biblically depicted as 400 plus years of slavery? Would not the Israelites have wanted to highlight their great rule of Egypt?

Older historical evidence certainly exists as to the rule of the Hyksos in Egypt. The **Royal Canon of Turin** is currently housed in the Museo Egizio, located in Torino (to which it owes its name). This papyrus is the best surviving chronology of the ancient Egyptian pharaohs. Unfortunately, it is greatly damaged.

Originally listing over 300 kings, it was written in a fine literate hand, around 1200 BC. Noted are the dynasties of the kings with the lengths of each reign in years, months and days. It also includes the names of ephemeral rulers, or those ruling over small territories that are barely known nowadays. These ephemeral rules have gone unmentioned in other sources.

Although they were not given cartouches, *the list includes the Hyksos rulers which were often left out of other lists of kings.*

Hieroglyphic signs were added to indicate that they were foreigners (Verso X, 21). Understandably so, the poor condition of the papyrus has made piecing the fragments together a nearly impossible task.[9]

There have been recent archaeological excavations to indicate that the process of immigration of the Hyksos was gradual as opposed to one of sudden and immediate force. An excavation around Tell ed–Daba displays a gradual Canaanite influence in the styles of pottery and architecture, for example, circa 1800 BC.[10] These current findings seem to explain Manetho's statement concerning Egypt, that the Hyksos, "easily conquered it by force, as we did not do battle against them."

Israel Finkelstein and Neil Asher Silberson, in their detailed archaeological study of the Hyksos, state that a far more trustworthy account than Manetho, who stated that the Hyksos were driven from Egypt and founded Jerusalem, is an Egyptian source of the sixteenth century BC which details the actions of Pharaoh Ahmose(s), of the Eighteenth Dynasty. It was he who sacked Avaris and chased the remnants of the Hyksos back to Canaan. They further utilize archaeological evidence, which collaborates with this document, to indicate that Avaris was abandoned *around* the middle of the sixteenth century (1500s) BC.[11]

In fact, a remarkable television special, **The Exodus Decoded**, produced by Simcha Jacobovici, dubbed "The Naked Archaeologist", co-produced by James

Cameron, of *Titanic* fame, concurs with the date of the Exodus as being around 1500 BC. In addition, he states the name of the pharaoh who chased them as being Ahmoses.

Basing his findings on seemingly insurmountable archaeological and scientific data, Jacobovici has presented evidence for belief that all of the ten plagues of Egypt could have well been caused by the Santorini volcanic eruption on a Greek island in the Aegeon Sea, often dated at circa 1630 BC, which he believes took place at this time, because of striking evidence tying it to the events of the exodus. The devastating eruption, which destroyed the Minoan civilization there, produced a series of minor eruptions. The study shows in detail, how these events could have indeed produced all of the plagues of Egypt.

In keeping, Ralph Ellis, author of *Tempest & Exodus*, further states that the *Tempest Stele* "was erected by the pharaoh Ahmose I at the beginning of the eighteenth dynasty of Egypt, or about 1570 BC" [12] in which are detailed the great storms that struck Egypt during his reign. Foster and Ritner of Yale University had completed a scientific paper entitled *Texts, Storms, and the Thera Eruption*, published in the *Journal of Near Eastern Studies* 55 (1): 1-14, which proved to be invaluable to Ellis' research, thereby equating both the volcanic eruption of Thera to the *Tempest Stele* as well as the biblical exodus.

The Bible records in Exodus 2:10 that Moses was adopted by the royal family of Egypt, which would have made him a prince. When he left the country after killing an Egyptian who was beating a Hebrew, he became disinherited by the royal family. According to Jacobovici, Ahmoses in Hebrew meant, "brother of Moses". All of a sudden it does not seem surprising that the Bible simply referred to him as "Pharaoh". Jacobovici, like Josephus and Ralph Ellis, views the Hyksos expulsion and the biblical exodus as being the same event. The Exodus Decoded is now available for viewing on YouTube. [13]

Knight and Lomas, in *The Hiram Key*, identify Sequenre Tao, an Egyptian king who was forced to live in Thebes during the Hyksos rule, as having been Hiram Abiff (see chapter ten). They further note his killer, or killers, as having been the Hyksos. Could the Egyptian whom Moses killed have been Sequenre?

It is in accordance with the fact that the mummy of Sequenre Tao suffered a violent death by a blow to the middle of his forehead, the same fate as proclaimed for Hiram in the famed Masonic legend, that they have been able to draw such a plausible comparison. In addition, they have also linked the Hyksos to the Israelites. [14] Throughout this book, the reader is presented with mounds of evidence that the Israelites may have been in Egypt at the time of the Hyksos reign. So much so, in fact, that their claim seems irrefutable.

It would seem, however, that earlier archaeology and historical evidence, at least on the surface, disagree with their prospective on Hiram Abiff. In addition, the biblical account of the building of the temple in the Book of I Kings[15] tells us that construction began in the fourth year of Solomon's reign, thereby equating to 480 years after the exodus.

Based on a correlation of monarch reign dates, in keeping with both Egyptian and Assyrian sources, this would, then, date the exodus at around 1440 BC, more than 100 years *after* the expulsion of the Hysos from Egypt, proving what is already obvious: that the building of the Temple could not have taken place during the time of the Israelite stay in Egypt.

According to Knight and Lomas, however, the building of the Temple does not have to correspond with Hiram Abiff. The theory they propose in *The Hiram Key* states that it was Joseph's estimated rise to power that gives logical estimations of ages and, would, therefore, correspond precisely to the dates of Hyksos reign.

Based on to the first chapter of the Book of Exodus[16], these dates have been highly debated, especially as the children of Israel are depicted as being forced to build a city, most commonly identified with the city of Pi-Ramses, built in the delta just north of the site of Avaris, during the reign of Ramses II (c. 1279 to 1213 BC). Due to great dispute over this theory, many have abandoned it. In addition, Finkelstein and Silberman have shared that the first mention of Israel in the extra-biblical text was found in Egypt in **the stele describing the actions of Pharaoh Merneptah, son of Ramses II,** at the end of the thirteenth century BC, a fact that has been deemed most significant.

In this text, Merneptah declared that Egypt had conducted a destructive campaign into Canaan, while bragging about the people of Israel, "their seed is not!" This arrogant boast, of a king wanting to claim supremacy, could only have applied to their presence in Egypt, for there is indication that settlements of Israelites were in Canaan at that time. While there is no mention of Israel in any documents of the Hyksos period, one of the later *el-Amarna Letters* of the fourteenth century BC does indicate that Canaan was a possession of Egypt, and their kings in subjection.[17]

Although Finkelstein and Silberman have trouble finding proof of both Israelite slavery and the exodus of Israel from Egypt, they have dated the Hyksos presence long before that of the Israelites, going so far as to say that Egyptian names and background in the story of Joseph were more prominent in the seventh century BC.[18] While this conclusion may seem rash, even Knight and Lomas agree that some of the items mentioned in the biblical narrative of Joseph were outside of the depicted time frame of the era of the Hyksos rule, therefore concluding that the biblical account could have been written much later.[19] It is quite possible that the verbiage in the manuscripts was altered from earlier texts, making it appear to be out of time sequence with the actual events.

The fact that there is no mention of Israel, Joseph or Moses in the Egyptian records, by these same names, does not surprise me in the least. The name of Hatshepsut, the female pharaoh (fifth pharaoh of the Eighteenth Dynasty c. 1473-1458 BC), is not mentioned on the King List. Her step-son/nephew, Tuthmosis III, would have had her blotted from history.

A minor at the time of his pharaoh father's death, after becoming of age, he grew jealous of his step-mother. Following her sudden disappearance, he immediately took over the throne, removing her name from the annals of Egypt.[20] Such is the face of jealousy.

Who, then, were the Hyksos? Though many now hold the view that they were the Israelites themselves, it seems fairly certain to me that they were the Edomites, cousins of the Israelites, the descendants of Jacob's twin brother, Esau.

A book first published in 1962, written by David J. Gibson, titled *Whence Came the Hyksos Kings of Egypt* (mentioned briefly in chapter three), is now available online, chronicling a number of points, in fifteen chapters, all evidence from scripture, history and archaeology, stating reasons for the conclusions reached therein.[21]

Gibson believed that the Israelites were slaves in Egypt during the Hyksos reign, and that the pharaoh who reigned at the time of the Exodus, who "knew not Joseph", seems to have been "the founder [Ahmoses] or an early king of the powerful 18th dynasty (1546-1319 BC)."[22] However, these dates are somewhat questionable.

After reviewing all of the evidence on this, please take the time to consider the following facts.

1) The biblical story of Joseph states that when his brothers sold him into slavery he was purchased by the "Ishmaelites". [23]

2) Ishmaelites were the descendants of Ishmael, the son of Abraham by Hagar, the Egyptian handmaid of Sarah.

3) The Hyksos were very probably Edomites, descendants of Esau, who were elaborated upon in the previous chapter, immediately prior to the story of Joseph in the Book of Genesis.

4) An enormous amount of evidence points to the Hyksos presence in Egypt during the same time frame as the Israelites.

It seems both highly plausible and probable that all of the parties involved were likely Hebrews, descendants of Abraham. It is my belief that the Canaanite-Edomite Hyksos King who exalted Joseph to power was acceptant of him because he knew that Joseph was a relative. This scenario presents just one more cause for angst between the various branches of Abrahamic faith.

Chapter 5 Footnotes

[1]Egyptology Online.com (2008). *Manetho and the King List*. Retrieved February 2008 from http://www.egyptologyonline.com/manetho.htm
[2]Finkelstein, Israel and Silberman, Neil Asher. (2001). *The Bible Unearthed* (p 55). The Free Press, New York, NY.
[3]Rohl, David M. (1995). *A Test of Time: The Bible from Myth to History* (p 312). Bohemian Books of London: London, UK.
[4]Wiston, William. (1987). *The Works of Josephus, Complete and Unabridged* (p 778). Hendrickson Publishers: Peabody, MA as taken from Flavius Josephus, *Against Apion*, Book 1.73
[5]Knight, Christopher, and Robert, Lomas. (2001). *The Hiram Key* (pp 124, 125, 127). Fair Winds Press, Glouchester, MA.[6]Wiston, William. (1987). *The Works of Josephus, Complete and Unabridged* (p 779). Hendrickson Publishers: Peabody, MA as taken from Flavius Josephus, *Against Apion*, Book 1.14.87
[7]Ibid, sections 88-90
[8]Ibid, sections 91-92
[9]Egyptology Online.com (2008). *Manetho and the King List*. Retrieved February 2008 from http://www.egyptologyonline.com/manetho.htm
[10]Finkelstein, Israel and Silberman, Neil Asher. (2001). *The Bible Unearthed* (pp 54-55). The Free Press, New York, NY.
[11]Ibid, p 55
[12]Ellis, Ralph. (2000). *Tempest & Exodus* (p 47). Adventures Unlimited: Kempton, IL.

[13]Simcha Jacobovici. *The Exodus Decoded.* Retrieved March 2008 from the YouTube website located at http://www.youtube.com/watch?v=VBBvvDl25F4

[14]Knight, Christopher, and Robert, Lomas. (2001). *The Hiram Key* (pp 124, 125, 127, 130). Fair Winds Press, Glouchester, MA.

[15]I Kings 6:1

[16]Exodus 1:11

[17]Bible History Online (2007). *El-Armana Letters.* Retrieved February 2008 from http://www.bible-history.com/archaeology/israel/el-amarna-letters.html

[18]Finkelstein, Israel and Silberman, Neil Asher. (2001). *The Bible Unearthed* (pp 54-67). The Free Press, New York, NY.

[19]Knight, Christopher, and Robert, Lomas. (2001). *The Hiram Key* (p 130). Fair Winds Press, Glouchester, MA.

[20]Wood, Mike and Wood, Janet. (1995) *Ancient Egyptian Female Pharaohs* – Hatshepsut. Retrieved February 2008 from Ancient Egypt and Ancient Egyptians MultimediaWebsite located at http://www.ancientnile.co.uk/pharaohs-women.php

[21]Gibson, David J. *The Hyksos, Kings of Egypt and the land of Edom, Chapter VII, Religion and Date of the Edomite Empire.* Retrieved February 2008 from http://nabataea.net/edomch7.html

[22]Ibid, *Chapter 1, The Enormous Hyksos Empire.* http://nabataea.net/edomch1.html

[23]Genesis 37:28

[24]Genesis 36:8

JOSEPH IS MADE RULER OVER EGYPT.

Joseph is Made Ruler over Egypt
(artist unknown)
(from *Stories of the Bible* by Charles Foster)

Chapter Six
Og, King of Bashan
And Other Post-Flood Giants

Og, the king of the biblical Bashan, east of Jordan, whom the Israelites conquered while journeying to occupy the "promised land", is mentioned in scriptures seventeen times. This is more than any other conquered foe.

What was so unusual about Og? He was a giant of the race known as Rephaim (רפאים). His iron bed was recorded as being thirteen feet, six inches long, and six feet wide.[1]

Josephus tells the story like this:

"When matters were come to this state, Og, the king of Gilead and Gaulanitis, fell upon the Israelites. He brought an army with him, and in haste to the assistance of his friend Sihon: but though he found him already slain, yet did he resolve still to come and fight the Hebrews, supposing he should be too hard for them, and being desirous to try their valor; but failing of his hope, he was both himself slain in the battle, and all his army was destroyed. So Moses passed over the river Jabbok, and overran the kingdom of Og. He overthrew their cities, and slew all their inhabitants, who yet exceeded in riches all the men in that part of the continent, on account of the goodness of the soil, and the great quantity of their wealth. Now Og had very few equals, either in the largeness of his body, or handsomeness of his appearance. He was also a man of great activity in the use of his hands, so that his actions were not unequal to the vast largeness and handsome appearance of his body. And men could easily guess at his strength and magnitude when they took his bed at Rabbath, the royal city of the Ammonites; its structure was of iron, its breadth four cubits, and its length a cubit more than double thereto. However, his fall did not only improve the circumstances of the Hebrews for the present, but by his death he was the occasion of further good success to them; for they presently took those sixty cities, which were encompassed with excellent walls, and had been subject to him, and all got both in general and in particular a great prey."[2]

Who were the Rephaim? The word means "lofty men". They were a race of giants who occupied a valley in the kingdom of the Amorites, called "the land of the giants" in the Old Testament,[3] in the time of the exodus of the Jews from Egypt, around the fifteenth century BC. It is thought, by some, that both the Rephaim and the Anakim, another pre-Canaanite tribe of the area mentioned in the biblical books of Numbers, Deuteronomy, Joshua and Judges, were survivors of the Nephilim.[4]

When Joshua sent spies into Caanan after the death of Moses, they reported, "We saw the Nephilim there (the descendants of Anak come from the Nephilim). We seemed like grasshoppers in our own eyes, and we looked the same to them."[5]

If the flood of Noah destroyed all other life on earth besides Noah's family, how were there still Nephilim after the exodus from Egypt?

Conversely, many commentators feel that the spies exaggerated the size of the "giants", based on the smaller size of the Israelites.

One thing is for certain, the spies were familiar with the Nephilim, believing that they still existed. While all versions of the Bible appear to use the term "sons of Anak", in the first chapter of Deuteronomy, they are called "sons of Anakim".[6]

When reflecting upon the numerous biblical references regarding tribes of giants in the post-flood era, a most curious fact soon became evident to me. In identifying all other surrounding tribes as the descendants of *men*, as per the ***Tanakh***, or Old Testament, the suffix used with the ancestor's name was "ites". The descendants of Israel became known as Israelites. Other tribes included the Ammonites, the Hittites, the Amalakites, the Jebusites, the Hivites, the Arkites, the Sinites, and Israel's cousins, the Ismaelites, the Edomites, and the Moabites. This list is clearly not exhaustive. It was *only* when referring to the tribes of giants that the plural masculine noun suffix used is "im", which is also applied in reference to the plural word for deity, Elohim.

Ancient rabbis stated in the ***Babylonian Talmud*** that the Rephaim giants, Sihon, king of Amorites, and Og, king of Bashan, were grandsons of a fallen angel named Shamhazai.[7] This conclusion, of course, would assume survival of the pre-flood Nephilim.

There is a passage from the *Midrash* which describes a legend of Noah saving Og. "As the floodwaters swelled, Og, king of Bashan, sat himself on one of the rungs of the ark's ladders and swore to Noah and to his sons that he would be their slave forever. What did Noah do? He punched a hole in the ark, and through it he handed out food to Og every day. Og's survival, or that of his line, is hinted at in the verse 'Only Og remained of the remnant of the Rephaim' (Deuteronomy 3:11)."[8]

In the *Midrash Rabbah*, an amplification of the Torah, the size of Og seems to have become more exaggerated than ever. Rabbi Johanan wrote: "The length of his feet was eighteen cubits. Thereupon Moses became frightened, but God said, 'Do not fear, because I will make him fall before you.'"[9] Eighteen cubits would equate to twenty-seven feet. At this rate, Og could have been two hundred feet tall.

Though Og was said to be the last survivor of his particular race of giants, Josephus later says of the time after Joshua: "There were till then left the race of giants, who had bodies so large, and countenances so entirely different from other men, that they were surprising to the sight, and terrible to the hearing. The bones of these men are still shown to this very day".[10] His day, of course, was the first century of the current Christian era.

These giants certainly seemed to be very dissimilar from the Adamic race. According to various books and Internet reports, many skeletal remains of pre-historic giants have been unearthed, a number of them in the Western Hemisphere. Some were said to be up to twelve feet tall.[11] To have one of them tested for DNA purposes would be both interesting and historic. If, indeed, this has already been done, the results, to my knowledge, have not been made public.

It has been voiced that the Nephilim and the Neanderthal could be one and the same,[12] although I am very skeptical. The DNA extracted from bones is always mitochondrial, indicating direct maternal origins. Many ancient texts telling of Nephilim state that these hybrids were sired by another race known as "sons of God", as stated in chapter two. The mothers were fully human. Maternal DNA, therefore, would merely lead us back to the original female ancestor, showing up as human rather than non-human, as is the case with Neanderthals. Genetic research is proving to be a fascinating science, in that it is constantly revealing new avenues of discovering our past, while gazing directly into the probabilities of our future.

Og, like Goliath, the giant Philistine in the later day of David, became an icon of the power of Yahweh to lead the nation of Israel on to victory.

Chapter 6 Footnotes

[1]Deuteronomy 3:11
[2]Wiston, William. (1987). *The Works of Josephus, Complete and Unabridged* (p 108). Hendrickson Publishers: Peabody, MA as taken from Flavius Josephus, *Antiquities of the Jews*, Book 4.5.3 (96).
[3]Deuteronomy 3:13
[4]Geerts, L.C. (2008). *Chapter 5: Giants, Nephilim and Anakim*. Retrieved February 2008 from Earth's Ancient History website located at http://www.earth-history.com/Earth-05.htm
[5]Numbers 13:33, NIV
[6]Deuteronomy 1:28, NIV
[7]*Babylonian Talmud: Tractate Niddah* Folio 6la. Retrieved March 2008 from http://www.come-and-hear.com/niddah/niddah_61.html
[8]Gluskin, Rabbi Shai. (2007). *Midrash on Noah and Og*. Retrieved February 2008 from Jewish Reconstructionist Federation website located at http://www.jrf.org/showres&rid=66
[9]Kahn, Rabbi Ari. (2007). *Og*. Retrieved February 2008 from Weekly Torah Portion as located at http://www.aish.com/torahportion/moray/Og.asp
[10] Wiston, William. (1987). *The Works of Josephus, Complete and Unabridged* (p 135). Hendrickson Publishers: Peabody, MA as taken from Flavius Josephus, *Antiquities of the Jews*, Book 5.2.3 (125).
[11]Martinez, Pablo L. (2006). *Giant Remains of the Nephilim – What Darwinian "Scientists" do not Want you to Know*. Retrieved February 2008 from http://www.returnofthenephilim.com/GiantBonesDiscoveries.html

[12]*Neanderthal and Nephilim – One and the Same?*
Retrieved February 2008 from The Age of Giants
website located at
http://www.geocities.com/age_of_giants/ancient_gi
ants/neanderthal.html

Chapter Seven
Rahab

The riddle of Rahab is not so much who she was, but why she was plummeted to fame in the annals of Israel. Her saga begins to unfold, much like a Shakespearean play, in the second chapter of the Book of Joshua. Moses is dead and Joshua (Hebrew יְהוֹשֻׁעַ Yehoshua) is the newly appointed savior of the children of Israel. The time for which they had long awaited has finally arrived. While camped at Shittim, in the Jordan valley, he sends two spies across the river to Jericho to investigate the military preparedness of the city while also clearing the way for the invasion of Canaan.

Where should these brave men arrive first, but at the home of a prostitute whose house was on the city wall. From the account in Joshua, it appears that they didn't just arrive and leave. The Bible says that "they lodged there" [1], staying long enough that news of their arrival, as well as the purpose of their stay, got back to the king. When asked by the soldiers to state the location of the spies, Rahab lied, saying that they had left. In keeping, this foreign prostitute who lied became a hero of Israel, and an ancestor in the line of Jesus. Why?

We get the rest of the story from Josephus, who identifies her home as an inn; hence, she is merely the inn keeper. More detail is given to the actual location of the inn, being where they went to eat their supper, and indicating that after the meal they were wondering how to get away.

Josephus shares that the king was informed of their whereabouts, that same night, as he dined, and that "he sent immediately some to them, and commanded to catch them, and bring them to him, that he might examine them by torture, to learn what their business was there."[2] A slightly different angle to the story emerges

When Rahab heard that the spies were being sought out by the king, she hid them within the stalks of flax lying on the roof of her house, drying after harvest, thus saving their lives and allowing them to escape.

Rahab took a considerable chance in hiding the spies, punishable by death. She acknowledged the God of the Hebrews, saying, "I know that the Lord hath given you the land, and that your terror is fallen upon us, and that all the inhabitants of the land faint because of you. For we have heard how the Lord dried up the Red Sea for you, when you came out of Egypt; and what ye did unto the two kings of the Amorites, that were on the other side of Jordan, Sihon and Og, whom ye utterly destroyed. And as soon as we had heard *these things* our hearts did melt, neither did there remain any more courage in any man, because of you: for the Lord your God, he is God in heaven above, and in earth beneath. Now therefore, I pray you, swear unto me by the Lord, since I have showed you kindness, that ye will also show kindness unto my father's house, and give me a true token: and that ye will save alive my father and my mother, and my brethren, and my sisters, and all that they have, and deliver our lives from death."[3]

Her confession of faith in the God of Israel, her plea for salvation from death, her daring act (risking her own life in order to save the soldiers assigned to the spying), all resulted in Rahab and her entire household being spared. According to her agreement with the spies, she bound a "line of scarlet thread" in the window from which she let them down so that they could escape outside the city wall.

Rahab then became a part of the nation of Israel, converting to Judaism and marrying a member of the tribe of Judah, named Salmon, thus becoming the mother of Boaz, who married Ruth, another foreigner who voluntarily left her people to follow Yahweh. Boaz and Ruth were the parents of Obed, the father of Jesse, the father of King David.

She is listed both in Hebrews, chapter eleven, verse twenty-one, as a person of great faith, and in James 2:25, as an example of good works.

Chapter 7 Footnotes

[1]Joshua 1:1
[2]Wiston, William. (1987). *The Works of Josephus, Complete and Unabridged* (p 128). Hendrickson Publishers: Peabody, MA as taken from Flavious Josephus, *Antiquities of the Jews,* Book 5.1.7 and 5.1. 8
[3]Joshua 2:8-13

Rahab by Maerten deVos

Chapter Eight
The Witch of Endor

Another more mysterious and controversial person in the Old Testament was called "the Witch of Endor". Her entry into the canon scriptures occurs due to the fact that she was consulted by King Saul, the first true king of the nation of Israel. According to scholars, this incident took place about 1053 BC. Under the laws of the Jewish people, they were strictly forbidden from consulting "soothsayers" or "familiar spirits". Sorcery, witchcraft, and attempts to consult the dead were considered taboo.[1] Even so, there was no attempt made to cover up this story, unveiled in the First Book of Samuel, and the twenty-eighth chapter.

Samuel the Prophet, who had both anointed Saul king and had served as his counselor in spiritual matters, died. "And Saul had put away those who had familiar spirits, and the wizards out of the land".[2] But the Philistines had gathered together an army to attack him. Saul was terrified; as their army greatly outranked his own. Being so far removed from communication with God, he had received no response from the efforts of the prophets, dreams, nor his own inner feelings.[3] Clearly, he was desperate enough to try anything.

7. "Then Saul said unto his servants, Seek me a woman that hath a familiar spirit, that I may go to her, and enquire of her. And his servants said unto

him, Behold there is a woman that hath a familiar spirit in Endor.

8. And Saul disguised himself, and put on other raiment, and he went, and the two men with him, and they came to the woman by night: and he said, I pray thee, divine unto me by the familiar spirit, and bring me *him up*, whom I shall name unto thee.

9. And the woman said unto him, Behold thou knowest what Saul hath done, how he hath cut off those that have familiar spirits, and the wizards, out of the land; wherefore then layest thou a snare for my life, to cause me to die?

10. And Saul sware to her by the Lord, saying, As the Lord liveth, there shall no punishment happen to thee for this thing.

11. Then said the woman, Whom shall I bring up unto thee? And he said, Bring me up Samuel.

12. And when **the woman saw Samuel**, she cried with a loud voice: and the woman spake to Saul, saying, Why hast thou deceived me? For thou art Saul.

13. And the king said unto her, Be not afraid: for what sawest thou? And the woman said unto Saul, **I see gods ascending out of the earth.**

14. And the king said unto her, What form is he of? And she said, An old man cometh up; and he *is*

covered with a mantle. **And Saul perceived that it was Samuel**, and he stooped with *hi*s face to the ground, and bowed himself.

15. And **Samuel said to Saul**, Why hast thou disquieted me, to bring me up? And Saul answered, I am sore distressed; for the Philistines make war against me, and God departed from me, and answerest me no more, neither by prophets, nor by dreams; therefore I have called thee, that thou mayest make known unto me what I shall do.

16. **Then said Samuel**, Wherefore then doest thou ask of me, seeing the Lord is departed from thee, and is become thine enemy?

17. And the Lord hath done to him, as he spake by me; for the Lord hath rent the kingdom out of thy hand, and given it to thy neighbor, *even* to David:

18. Because thou obeyedst not the voice of the Lord, nor executedst his fierce wrath upon Amalek, therefore hath the Lord done this thing unto thee this day.

19. Moreover the Lord will also deliver Israel with thee into the hand of the Philistines.

20. Then Saul fell straightway all along on the earth, and was sore afraid, because of **the words of Samuel:** and there was no strength in him; for he had eaten no bread that day, nor all the night."

The woman saw that Saul was both greatly troubled and hungry. Knowing that she had done all that he had asked, indeed even risking her own life, she requested that he allow her to do one more thing for him: "set a morsel of bread before him" so that he might eat for the strength required of his journey home. He refused, and yet his servants also plead with him, leading the woman to kill her "fatted calf" in order to feed the king and his servants.

The story continues, with David meeting the Philistines. The situation comes to a head in the thirty-first, and final, chapter of I Samuel.

"Now the Philistines fought against Israel: and the men of Israel fled from before the Philistines, and fell slain in mount Gilboa.

"And the Philistines followed hard upon Saul and upon his sons; and the Philistines slew Jonathan, and Abinadab, and Melchishua, Saul's sons. And the battle went sore against Saul, and the archers hit him; and he was wounded of the archers.

"Then said Saul unto his armourbearer, Draw thy sword, and thrust me through therewith; lest these uncircumcised come and thrust me through, and abuse me. But his armourbearer would not; for he was sore afraid. Therefore Saul took a sword and fell upon it."[4]

Who was the witch of Endor? Was she really able to conjure the spirit of Samuel? The latter has been a hard matter of dispute in Christian circles.

Both early Church fathers, and conservative believers alike, have debated whether the "spirit" was that of Samuel. Some teach that it was a demon spirit who merely took his shape. The Hebrew word translated "gods" in verse thirteen is *elohim*. In the 1985 version of the *Tanakh*, this is translated as "a divine messenger". The Living Bible says, "a specter". All translations say that it was Samuel, including the Jewish *Tanakh*.

As to the identity of the "witch", though her name is never mentioned in scripture, the Jewish rabbinical *Midrash* maintains that she was Zephaniah, the mother of Abner, son of Nur, a cousin of Saul, and commander of his army.[5]

Necromancers, sometimes identified as witches, wizards and the like, have commonly claimed these same abilities throughout history. It is here that this woman, who would have otherwise faded into oblivion, is immortalized, all due to the fear and desperation of an alarmed king.

Is it possible that a real specter might have been brought to life in this case? Or is it as equally plausible that the "spirit" may have been the mere imagination, or falsification, of a woman who was more afraid at the prospect of not being able to produce the dead prophet for the desperate king?

Christians and Jews alike consider this book an inspired writing, worthy of their canon. Five separate verses go on to identify this spirit as being "Samuel".

The Jewish religion does not deny the reality of this appearance of Samuel. According to Rabbis, the spirit still hovers near the body after death. One example in the *Midrash Rabbah* is that of Bar Kappara. He taught: "Until three days [after death] the soul keeps on returning to the grave, thinking that it will go back [into the body]; but when it sees that the facial features have become disfigured, it departs and abandons it [the body]." [6]

Verse twelve states, "... the woman **saw Samuel**". Verse fourteen says, "Saul **perceived** that it **was** Samuel. The *Tanakh* uses the statement, "Saul **knew** that it was Samuel. Verse fifteen reads, "Then **Samuel said**", and in verse sixteen, "Then **said Samuel**". Verse twenty identifies the message delivered as "**the words of Samuel**".

Nowhere in any of these cited scriptures does it make any variation from this claim, the statements that Samuel actually spoke to Saul. In addition, nowhere does it say that the words were delivered from the mouth of the woman known as the "witch of Endor", as some are sure to say.

The words spoken by the "spirit" all rang true, with his predictions coming to pass exactly as they were foretold. According to scripture, the test of a prophet lies in the truth of the message.

In the Hebrew it states "there is a woman *Behabalth-Ob*". This may be translated *python,* or *one owning a python or contacting evil spirits.* It may also be "*One who possesses a talisman*". It is most likely that they saw her as possessing a talent to consult with the dead through magic, seen as evil in the sight of Yahweh.

From the demeanor of the "witch", it seems that she was just as terrified and surprised, as was Saul, by the appearance of the spirit identified as Samuel.

Some see this passage as a satire on Saul, a man who was once favored by God, now driven to desperation by his own demons.

The story is also related by Josephus, who wrote that "his form was like a god", while identifying him as actually being the spirit of Samuel, brought up from "hades", the word used at that time for the abode of the dead.[7]

Chapter 8 Footnotes

[1]Leviticus 20:27
[2]I Samuel 28:3
[3]I Samuel 28:4-5
[4]I Samuel 31:1-4
[5]Hirsch, Emil G. *The Witch of Endor*. Retrieved March 2008 from JewishEncyclopedia.com at http://www.jewishencyclopedia.com/view.jsp?letter=E&artid=366
[6]Komarnitsky, Kris. (2005). *Souls, Decay, 3 Day, and Methodology*. Retrieved March 2008 from XTalk: Historical Jesus and Origins Yahoo Group located at http://groups.yahoo.com/group/crosstalk2/message/19949
[7]Wiston, William. (1987). *The Works of Josephus, Complete and Unabridged* (p 177). Hendrickson Publishers: Peabody, MA as taken from Flavious Josephus, *Antiquities of the Jews*, Book 6.14.2 (333)

**The Ghost of Samuel Speaking to Saul
by Jilius Schnorr von Carolsfeld**

Chapter Nine
The Queen of Sheba

The renowned "queen of the south[1]", as she was called by Jesus, is the stuff legends are made of. Her story, as told in I and II Kings in the *Tanakh*, or Old Testament, still flourishes today. Her legend is alive throughout Arabia, Iraq, Israel and Ethiopia, in the *Qur'an* as well as Arabian folklore, which spins more modern tales involving magic carpets, talking birds, and mystical transportation. In addition, there are several Jewish legends that present dubious accounts of the famed queen with Solomon.

The first mention of the name "Sheba", which occurs in Genesis chapter twenty-five, was of a grandson of Abraham by Katurah, the son of their son, Jokshan. Most likely, he was the father of people bearing this name.[2]

In I Chronicles, chapter one, it is written that Noah's grandson, Cush, the son Ham, and father of the famous Nimrod, also had a son named Seba, It has been thought by some scholars that Seba was the founder of this tribe.[3] Another of Ham's sons was Canaan, for which this nation was named. The same chapter, however, later lists Sheba, the son of Jokshan.

The queen is introduced first in I Kings chapter ten: "And when the queen of Sheba heard of the fame of Solomon concerning the name of the LORD, she came to prove him with hard questions. And she came to Jerusalem with a very great train, with camels that bare spices, and very much gold, and precious stones: and when she was come to Solomon, she communed with him of all that was in her heart. And Solomon told her all her questions: there was not *any* thing hid from the king, which he told her not. And when the queen of Sheba had seen all Solomon's wisdom, and the house that he had built, And the meat of his table, and the sitting of his servants, and the attendance of his ministers, and their apparel, and his cupbearers, and his ascent by which he went up unto the house of the LORD; there was no more spirit in her. And she said to the king, It was a true report that I heard in mine own land of thy acts and of thy wisdom. Howbeit I believed not the words, until I came, and mine eyes had seen *it:* and, behold, the half was not told me; thy wisdom and prosperity exceedeth the fame which I heard. Happy *are* thy men, happy *are* these thy servants, which stand continually before thee, *and* that hear thy wisdom. Blessed be the LORD thy God, which delighted in thee, to set thee on the throne of Israel: because the LORD loved Israel for ever, therefore made he thee king, to do judgment and justice. And she gave him an hundred and twenty talents of gold, and of spices very great store, and precious stones: there came no more such abundance of spices as these which the queen of Sheba gave to king Solomon. And the navy also of Hiram, that brought gold from Ophir, brought in from Ophir great plenty of almug trees, and precious stones. And the king made of the almug trees pillars for the house of the LORD, and for the kings house, harps also and psalteries for singers: there came no such almug trees, nor were seen unto this day. And king Solomon gave unto the queen of Sheba all her desire, whatsoever she asked, beside *that* which Solomon gave her of his royal bounty. So she turned and went to her own country, she and her servants."[4]

Though her name is not mentioned in the Bible, there is a Muslim tradition that it was Balkis. Josephus called her the "Queen of Egypt and Ethiopia"[5], but it is now most commonly believed that the kingdom over which she reigned was likely Arabia and/or Ethiopia.

In both the biblical text and the historical account of Josephus, the attraction and magnetism which the queen felt for Solomon is undeniable. Josephus says, "Now when the queen had demonstrated how deeply the king had affected her, her disposition was known by certain presents..." Josephus further states, "There was nothing that she desired which he denied her."[6]

The *Kebra Negast*, "The Book of the Glory of the Kings", the holy book of Ethiopian Christians and Jamaican Rastafarians, contains a detailed drama of the Queen of Sheba and Solomon, said to have been passed down through the generations. The tablets, written in Ethiopic text, dated by contemporary scholars to the fourteenth century, were first translated into English and published in 1922. They were received by many as a collection of legends and fables, but the book contains the story of the relationship between Solomon and the "Queen of Ethiopia", herein called "Makeda".

The queen was said to have learned of Solomon from Tamrin, the leader of her trade caravans. He allegedly brought gold, ebony and sapphires to Solomon for use in the building of the Temple by 700 carpenters and 800 stone masons.

There is a great deal written in the ***Kebra Negast*** about the conversations said to have taken place between this royal pair, the queen's deep affection for Solomon, and her subsequent conversion to Judaism.

According to this writing, after much time had passed, Solomon prepared an especially lavish feast for her, "And the royal meal had come to an end three times and seven times, and the administrators, and the counselors, and the young men and the servants had departed, and the King rose up and he went to the Queen, and he said unto her----now they were alone together----'Take thou thine ease here for love's sake until daybreak.' And she said unto him, 'Swear to me by thy God, the God of Israel, that thou wilt not take me by force. For if I, who according to the law of men am a maiden, be seduced, I should travel on my journey [back] in sorrow, and affliction and tribulation.'"[7]

More lengthy dialogue follows. She was to have been twenty-one, and a beautiful virgin. Eventually they are said to have slept together, after which he granted her leave to return to her kingdom. Shortly later, the book relates the birth of their son, Bayna-Leokem, also known as Menyelek I, or "Ibn-Hakim", which means, son of the wise man.

This story is accepted by millions as historical fact. He was said to have been crowned king of Ethiopia, and to have been called "David II". Not only is this a belief among Ethiopian Christians and Jamaican Rastafarians, but also Abyssinian Jews. A dynasty of uninterrupted royal Israeli-Ethiopian bloodline was certified by the Ethiopian Constitution in 1955. Members of a Jewish Temple there claim that it houses the Ark of the Covenant.

According to Ethiopian legend, the Queen of Sheba was born in Ophir about 1020 BC, but educated in Ethiopia. Her mother, so the story goes, was Queen Ismenie, and her father, chief minister to Za Sebado, succeeded him as king. Upon the death of her father, it is said that she ascended to the throne at the age of fifteen.

Chapter 9 Footnotes

[1]Matthew 12:42
[2]Genesis 25:3
[3]Gibson, David J. *The Founding of the Nations*. Retrieved February 2008 from http://nabataea.net/foundingnations.html
[4]I Kings 10: 1-13
[5]Wiston, William. (1987). *The Works of Josephus, Complete and Unabridged* (p 224). Hendrickson Publishers: Peabody, MA as taken from Flavious Josephus, *Antiquities of the Jews*, Book 8. 6.5 (165).
[6]Wiston, William. (1987). *The Works of Josephus, Complete and Unabridged* (p 225). Hendrickson Publishers: Peabody, MA as taken from Flavious Josephus, *Antiquities of the Jews*, Book 8.6.6 (175).
[7]The Kabra Negast 29. *The Narrative of Solomon and Queen Sheba continued*. Retrieved February 2008 from The Internet Sacred Text Archive located at http://www.sacred-texts.com/chr/kn/kn029.htm

THE QUEEN OF SHEBA.— *Cason &*

Depiction of the Queen of Sheba entering Israel
(artist not identified)

Chapter Ten
Hiram Abi(ff)

In I Kings 7:13, and later in II Chronicles 2:13, a man is introduced, subsequently viewed as the inspiration for "Hiram Abiff" in Masonic lore. Before this, in II Samuel 5:11, and I Kings 5:1-10, as well as in the proceeding verses on II Chronicles 2, a Hiram or Huram, King of Tyre, appears. A great admirer of King David, he is quick to lend help to Solomon in the building of the great Temple in Jerusalem, a building which had been previously envisioned by his father. The Hiram Abiff of Masonic lore has not been based on this biblical king, because a separate character appears in the Masonic drama which I shall discuss later, called "Hiram, King of Tyre".

The Hiram denoted within the I Kings record is called "a widow's son of the tribe of Naphtali". Interestingly enough, the Masonic character known as Hiram Abiff was also a widow's son.

In the account of II Chronicles 2:13, the King of Tyre is sending the second Huram (Hiram) to Solomon to assist in the building of the Temple. The king is quoted as referring to him as "a cunning man, endued with understanding, of Huram, my father's" (in Hebrew, Huram-Abi). According to *Strong's Concordance*, this word may also be translated "fatherless", which makes sense in this context.

He is further described as "The son of a woman of the daughters of Dan, and his father was a man of Tyre, skillful to work in gold, and in silver, in brass, and in iron, in stone, and in timber, in purple, in blue, and in fine linen, and in crimson; also to find out every devise which shall be put to him, with thy cunning men, and with the cunning men of David thy father." It is likely that his maternal grandmother was of the tribe of Dan, and his grandfather of Naphtali.

It is interesting to note that in the *Tanakh*, the books of the Chronicles do not appear immediately after the books of the Kings, as in the Christian Bible. In fact, they are not even in the *Nevi'im* at all, but are in the *Kethuvim*, as are other books which are placed in different order in the Christian "Old Testament". In fact, the Chronicles are the last books in the *Tanakh*. II Chronicles 2:12 in the *Tanakh* calls him "my master, Huram".

Said to have been the architect of Solomon's Temple, holding secrets used in its construction, three of his craftsmen threatened him in an attempt to force him to reveal these secrets. As their plot failed, Hiram is killed by three assassins, Julbela, Jubelo, and Jubelum, with a blow to his head. This story, highly revered by Freemasons, is considered by many to be symbolic of the high value placed on the preservation of secret knowledge.

With the birth of modern Freemasonry in 1717, the Hiram Abiff legend was not in use. However, by 1730, it was central to the practice in the Third Degree ritual[1], also known as Master Mason, which is the height and most sublime degree of the Craft.

The following detailed explanation of the Third Degree ceremony is based on ***Duncan's Masonic Ritual and Monito**r*, as published in 1866, a classic handbook through the ages. All direct quotes are from this source.

In the ritual, the candidate is stripped except for his shirt and underpants (traditionally long "drawers" were worn, and were rolled up to the knees). Both arms are removed from the shirt sleeves, leaving the candidate's arms and chest bare. A rope, called a cable-tow, is wound around the body three times, and a bandage, or hoodwink, is tied very closely over the eyes. The Deacon assigned leads him by the left arm up to the door of the Lodge and knocks three times loudly. The Senior Deacon, who has stationed himself at the inner door, at the right of the Senior Warden, then rises to his feet, makes the sign of a Master Mason to the Master, and addresses the Worshipful Master, thereby signifying the beginning of the ritual. The candidate must state that he is being submitted on his own free will. In addition, he must be vouched for, and found worthy.

After much ritualistic discourse, the blindfolded candidate kneels at an altar enhanced by three lamps. Placing his hands on the Bible, as well as the Masonic emblems of the square and compass, he takes the solemn oath of the Master Mason. In this vow he swears that he will "always hail, ever conceal, and never reveal any of the secrets, arts, parts, point or points, of the Master Masons' Degree, to any person or persons whomsoever, except it be to a true and lawful brother of this Degree, or in a regularly constituted Lodge of Master Masons." Much ritualistic dialogue is repeated. Also used are the password and the grip of the Master Mason, including the raps of the gavel.

After much discourse, the candidate is presented with the apron and tools of the Master Mason, and dressed.

Finally, the Worshipful Master tells the candidate that he is not yet a Master Mason, nor does he know that he ever will be, until he knows if he "can withstand the trials and dangers" that await him.

The candidate kneels once more. The conductor ties the blindfold tighter, so he can see nothing.

After the candidate has said "Amen", and the Lodge room has been darkened by turning down the lamps, the conductor takes the candidate by the right arm. Helping him up, they proceed to travel three times around the room, as with the path of the sun. As they start, the conductor begins to relate the following to the candidate:

"Brother, it was the usual custom of our Grand Master, Hiram Abiff" (the first he hears about

Hiram Abiff), "to enter into the unfinished 'Sanctum Sanctorum, or Holy of Holies,' of King Solomon's Temple, each day at high twelve, while the crafts were called from labor to refreshment, for the purpose of drawing out his designs upon the trestle-board, whereby the crafts might pursue their labors; after which, it was further his custom to offer up his devotions to the Deity. Then he would retire at the south gate of the outer courts of the Temple; and, in conformity with the custom of our Grand Master, whose memory we all so reverently adore, we will now retire at the south gate of the Temple."

At this point, they have passed around the Lodge three times. As they approach the Junior Warden's station in the south, he steps silently out from his seat to the floor whereby he confronts the blindfolded candidate, grabbing him by the collar very harshly, while exclaiming: (as Jubela, First Ruffian) "Grand Master Hiram, I am glad to meet you thus alone. I have long sought this opportunity. You will remember you promised us that when the Temple was completed, we should receive the secrets of a Master Mason, whereby we might travel in foreign countries, work, and receive Master's wages. Behold! The Temple is now about to be completed, and we have not obtained that which we have so long sought. At first, I did not doubt your veracity; but now I do! (He now gives the candidate a sudden twitch by the collar.) I therefore now demand of you the secrets of a Master Mason!"

The conductor then speaks for the candidate, stating that after the Temple is finished, if he is worthy, he will then receive the secrets of the Master Mason, but not before.

The Junior Warden, as Jubela, shakes the candidate, demanding that he tell the secrets, promising to take his life if he fails to comply.

The conductor again speaks for the candidate, stating that they cannot be given except in the presence of Solomon, the King of Tyre, and himself.

The confrontation continues more fiercely. The Ruffian brushes the candidate's throat with his right hand, while letting go of his grip with his left hand.

The Senior Warden then enters as the Second Ruffian, demanding the secrets of the candidate even more harshly. The conductor continues his refusals, in spite of another threat of murder.

After more ado, the Worshipful Master rejoins the play as the Third Ruffian, Jubelim, who is usually given a leather or "buckskin" bag stuffed with hair, which represents a "setting-maul". As the candidate is hurried toward him, the Worshipful Master seizes him. Placing his back near a canvas, he demands that he tell the secrets of the Master Mason. More threats and refusals occur, until the Worshipful Master says, "you have escaped 'Jubela' and 'Jubelo', but me you cannot escape...I hold in my hand an instrument of death..."

After another refusal uttered by the conductor, Jubelim exclaims, "Then die!" as he strokes him on the head with the bag, pushing him against the canvass. It is important to note, here, that a candidate is not actually harmed in any degree of Masonry.

It is then stated that he is dead, that his skull has been fractured. The identity of the candidate mysteriously becomes the Master, Hiram Abiff, and they reflect on not having received the secret knowledge. The question is then broached as to how they should dispose of the body. The Ruffians agree to place it in the rubbish of the Temple until "low twelve", before meeting to give it a decent burial.

After rolling the candidate up in the canvas, the three Ruffians tip-toe about in silence, until the Master strikes the hour of midnight on a bell or triangle. The Ruffians then cautiously approach the candidate, agreeing on where to bury "the body". The brethren carry the body around the Lodge and lower it "into the grave" (to the floor).

After a bit more conversation, one of the Ruffians suggests escaping the country. One of the brethren, portraying himself as a sea captain agrees to give them passage to Ethiopia, providing they have a pass from King Solomon. As they can present no pass, they are refused passage. They quickly state that they will acquire a pass, and return to the body.

Upon discussing their dilemma, they agree to flee to the interior of the country so as to avoid arrest. After going in various directions, the brethren jump up and start to laugh and sing.

They are soon called to order by the gavel of the Worshipful Master, now portraying King Solomon. He asks why the workmen are not busy.

"King Solomon" is told that there is no work laid out to be done, after which he inquires about the whereabouts of Hiram Abiff. He is told that Hiram has not been seen since noon of the day before, and that a diligent search has shown up nothing. Solomon calls forth an assembly of the craftsmen.

The rolls are called by the Secretary, who discovers that three "Ruffians" are missing. After reporting this to Solomon, twelve "Fellow Crafts" are admitted, all with important information to report concerning a conspiracy to take the life of Master Hiram Abiff. Fully acknowledging that they were with the three who committed the treacherous act of taking the Master's life, they plead their case, saying that they had recanted from the deed while the others persisted. They kneel, begging the pardon of the king.

At Solomon's bidding, they go forth in the four cardinal directions, searching for the Ruffians. They have also been told that if they do not locate the missing men, that they then must be punished for the crime.

Coming near the candidate, still rolled in the canvas, the Fellow Crafts sit down to rest. While debating what they should do, they suddenly notice that an acacia was pulled up, thereby exposing the newly dug "grave". A voice is heard. It is none other than that of Jubela, lamenting the act in which he participated. He is then joined by the other two, who also admit to their crime.

The Fellow Crafts are quick to seize the Ruffians, taking them before King Solomon so that they can tell their tale. All admit to their heinous crime. The king brings them to a speedy trial and each, in his order, pleads guilty. They are ordered to be executed immediately. A mock execution takes place, intended to make a great impression on the candidate.

King Solomon instructs the Fellow Crafts to find the body. They have been asked to determine if the Master's word, key, or anything pertaining to the Master's Degree is on, or about, the body.

Locating where the acacia was pulled up, they lift the canvas and pretend to dig up the body. They continue to search, not truly knowing what they are looking for. They find only "the jewel of his office" on a "yoke" tied around his neck, which they remove and take to Solomon.

The king sends them to exhume the body, and to the Treasurer, the King of Tyre, he proclaims, "My worthy brother of Tyre, as the Master's word is now lost, the first sign given at the grave, and the first word spoken, after the body is raised, shall be adopted for the regulation of all Masters' Lodges, until future generations shall find out the right."

A circle is formed around the body (candidate) and the Master, as Solomon, gives the sign of distress, and says, "O Lord my God, I fear the Master's word is forever lost!" At this point the whole company gathers and sings a solemn dirge. After another sign of distress from King Solomon, and repeating his previous statement of fear, he then turns to the Junior Warden, and says: "You will take the body by the Entered Apprentice grip, and see if it can be raised."[8]

After pretending to try, the Junior Warden tells the king that the body has been dead for fifteen days, and is too deteriorated to be raised.

Again the distress sign and repeated fear of the king that the Master's word is forever lost. Now he turns to the Senior Warden, portraying the King of Tyre, and repeats his plea. Still the body cannot be raised.

King Solomon then makes a brief plea to God for the dead son of the widow, again making the sign of distress. He turns to the King of Tyre, who suggests prayer. With all kneeling around the body, the Worshipful Master as Solomon recites the following prayer: "Thou, O God! knowest our down-sitting and our uprising, and understandest our thoughts afar off. Shield and defend us from the evil intentions of our enemies, and support us under the trials and afflictions we are destined to endure, while traveling through this vale of tears. Man that is born of a woman is of few days and full of trouble. He cometh forth as a flower, and is cut down: he fleeth also as a shadow, and continueth not. Seeing his days are determined, the number of his months are with thee; thou hast appointed his bounds that he cannot pass; turn from him that he may rest, till he shall accomplish his day. For there is hope of a tree, if it be cut down, that it will sprout again, and that the tender branch thereof will not cease. But man dieth and wasteth away; yea, man giveth up the ghost, and where is he? As the waters fail from the sea, and the flood decayeth and drieth up, so man lieth down, and riseth not up till the heavens shall be no more. Yet, O Lord! have compassion on the children of thy creation, administer them comfort in time of trouble, and save them with an everlasting salvation. Amen."

After asking that it may be so, all of the brethren rise. Solomon then asks for the assistance of the King of Tyre "to raise the body by the strong grip, or lion's paw, of the tribe of Judah".

The candidate is then raised, and given "the Grand Masonic word and the five points of fellowship," while the canvas is slipped out of the Lodge. When the secret word, which is said to be a substitute, since the first was lost in the death of Hiram Abiff, is whispered to the candidate, the blindfold is taken off, and he is pronounced a Master Mason.[2]

We have all heard the old adage, "giving him the third degree". Has not the origin of this saying become clearer to the reader? The detailed insight into this ritual, contained herein, was provided to show both the length and complexity of the heavily symbolic drama, as well as the purpose of the importance of Hiram Abiff, in Masonry. The ample setting demonstration in which he appears, in keeping with its relevance to the time of the building of Solomon's Temple, shows the importance of secret knowledge along with the ritualistic "raising of the dead". A great many references to, and some direct quotations from, the Bible are included in this rousing drama.

In the much-debated book by Christopher Knight and Robert Lomas, titled *The Hiram Key*,[3] a dissimilar Hiram emerges. Though both authors are Master Masons, their research led them to a strikingly radical conclusion. According to the book, Hiram Abiff lived five hundred years before the building of the first Temple in Jerusalem. They state that Egyptian Pharaoh Sequenenre Tao, whose life was at the end of the era of Hyksos' power in Egypt, fits the bill for the character of Hiram Abiff.

Knight and Lomas state that the Egyptians used a secret ceremony in the transition of power from one pharaoh to the next, thereby symbolizing death and resurrection. The authors also claim that drugs were used to make the pharaoh appear to die, during which it was claimed that he journeyed to the underworld to receive the power from the previous pharaoh. It was then that he was "resurrected", taking his place as a "god-king".

Knight and Lomas say that this practice dates from the early kingdom, when the two sections of Egypt were united. Their book goes on to share that when the Two Lands became one, they were symbolically joined by two pillars located at Thebes and Memphis. This concept of the two pillars lived on in King Solomon's Temple, as well as the Masonic Temples, which always feature pillars named Boaz and Jachin. Knight and Lomas are also of the belief that this story was passed down by Moses, who, raised as a prince in Egypt, was very aware of the ceremony.

A bit of a departure, Rosslyn Chapel, built in Midlothian Scotland in the fifteenth century, by Sir William St. Clair, as featured in *The Da Vinci Code*, contains three symbolic pillars. They are named the Apprentice Pillar, The Journeyman's Pillar, and The Master Mason's Pillar. Rosslyn has become the center of much discussion and debate, the subject of numerous books.

According to Knight and Lomas, the names of Solomon and Hiram were substituted in Masonic ceremony for the true Egyptian names. One thing is certain. Although the name Hiram Abiff is not mentioned in the Bible, per sé, his character will forever remain, at least as an allegorical icon, involved in the rituals of the Craft of Freemasonary. This has now been especially amplified by the tale unveiled from the minds of Knight and Lomas.

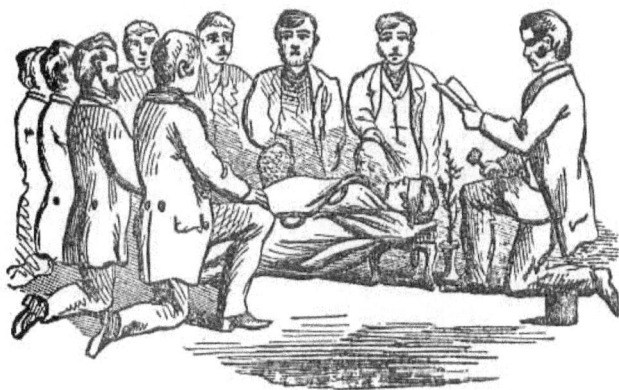

**Hiram Abiff is resurrected in the ritual of
the Master Mason
(from Duncan's Masonic Ritual)**

Chapter 10 Footnotes

[1]Bessel, Paul M. (1999). *The Hiram Abif legend in Freemasonry: What is it about? What are we supposed to learn from it?* Retrieved March 2008 from http://bessel.org/hiramab.htm
[2] Duncan, Malcolm C. (1866). *Duncan's Masonic Ritual and Monitor: Master Mason or Third Degree.* Retrieved March 2008 from The Internet Sacred Text Archive located at http://www.sacred-texts.com/mas/dun/dun04.htm
[3]Knight, Christopher and Lomas, Robert. (2001). *The Hiram Key* (pp 146-151). Fair Winds Press, Glouchester, MA.

Chapter Eleven
The Ten Lost Tribes of Israel

The story of Abram begins in Genesis chapter eleven. Verse thirty-two states that his father, Terah, took Abram, his wife, Sarai and his nephew, Lot, leaving their native home in Ur of the Chaldees (known as Persia in antiquity, but now known to be Iraq) to go to Canaan. It then follows with, "They came unto Haran and dwelt there", the last verse stating that Terah died there.

Chapter twelve begins, "Now the LORD had said unto Abram, Get thee out of thy country, and from thy kindred, and from thy father's house unto a land that I will shew thee. And I will make thee a great nation, and will bless thee, and make thy name great; and thou shalt be a blessing. I will bless them that bless thee, and curse them that curseth thee and in thee shall all the families of the earth be blessed."

Along the way, complications arose for Abram, the first being the split from his nephew, Lot, who then began living in Sodom. These complications soon became even more complex with the destruction of both Sodom and neighboring Gomorrah, after Abram had rescued him. However, it needs also to be remembered that Abram had another dilemma. He was a wealthy man, with no heirs, for his wife had been unable to bear him a child.

Chapter fifteen begins with, "After these things, the Word of the LORD came to Abram in a vision." A conversation is now recorded between Abram and God in the vision. Verse five reads: "and he (God) brought him forth abroad, and said, Look now toward heaven, and tell the stars, if thou be able to number them: And he said unto him, So shall thy seed be." But after ten years in Canaan, Sarai still remained barren.

Chapter sixteen tells the story of Sarai giving Hager, her Egyptian hand maid, to Abram, to bear a child for him. Thus, Ishmael was conceived, the first father of the Arab nations.

Chapter seventeen starts, "And when Abram was ninety years old and nine, the LORD appeared to Abram and said unto him, I am the Almighty God; (Hebrew, *El Shaddai*) walk before me, and be thou perfect. And I will make my covenant between me and thee, and will multiply thee exceedingly. And Abram fell on his face, and God talked with him saying, As for me, behold, my covenant is with thee, and thou shalt be a father of many nations. Neither shall thy name any more be called Abram (high father), but thy name shall be called Abraham (father of a multitude), for a father of many nations have I made thee. And I will and it shall be a token of the covenant make thee exceedingly fruitful, and I shall make nations of thee, and kings shall come out of thee. And I shall establish my covenant between me and thee, and thy seed after thee. And I will give unto thee and thy seed after thee, the land wherein thou art a stranger, all the land of Canaan, for an everlasting possession, and I will be their

God. And God said unto Abraham, Thou shalt keep my covenant therefore, thou, and thy seed after thee in their generations. This is my covenant, which ye shall keep, between me and you and thy seed after thee; Every man child among you shall be circumcised. And ye shall circumcise the flesh of your foreskin; and it shall be a token of the covenant betwixt me and you."

And beginning in verse fifteen, "And God said to Abraham, As for Sarai thy wife, thou shalt not call her name Sarai, but Sarah *shall* be her name. And I will bless her, and give thee a son also of her; yea, I will bless her and she shall be a *mother* of nations; kings of people shall be of her. Then Abraham fell upon his face, and laughed, and said in his heart, Shall a *child* be born unto him that is an hundred years old? And shall Sarah, that is ninety years old, bear? And Abraham said unto God, O that Ishmael might live before thee! And God said, Sarah thy wife shall bear thee a son indeed; and thou shalt call his name Issac (he laughed); and I will establish my covenant with him for an everlasting covenant, and with his seed after him. And as for Ishmael, I have heard thee; Behold, I have blessed him, and will make him fruitful, and will multiply him exceedingly, twelve princes shall he beget, and make him a great nation. **But my covenant shall I establish with Isaac, which Sarah shall bear unto thee** at this set time next year. And he left off talking from Abraham."

The majority of the natives of the nations which later came to be known as Israel and Judah in the Bible, were able to trace their ancestry to Isaac, and his son, Jacob, later called Israel. **Israel is to be the covenant people of God** according to *Genesis* sixteen.

The family of the elderly Jacob was moved to Egypt at the invitation of his son, Joseph, who, after being sold into slavery to the descendants of Ishmael by his jealous half-brothers, was providentially a ruler there, just under Pharaoh. This is believed to have occurred circa 2000-1700 BC.[1] According to the Bible, this move precipitated 400 years of Egyptian slavery, from which Moses (Hebrew *Moshe,* מֹשֶׁה) delivered the Israelites.

Following forty grueling years of wandering in the wilderness, the children of Israel were returned, under the leadership of Joshua, to their promised land about 1403 BC.[2] It is very interesting to note that while in Egypt, Israel grew to be a mighty nation. After the exodus, following a period of rule by judges, under the leadership of David and Solomon, their second and third kings, Israel reached its height of glorious power and world influence.

At varying times during the roller coaster ride of the history of Israel, their people have been divided, and some dispersion has occurred. The first true and great forced dispersion, however, took place in 721 BC, when Israel fell to the Assyrians. Just prior to

this, about 740, upon the fall of Damascus, Tiglath
Pileser III had carried Reuben, Gad, and the half
tribe of Manasseh into captivity in Mesopotamia.[3]

Between 597 and 581 BC, the fall of Judah occurred
before the attacks of Babylonia. The nations of
Israel and Judah, already divided since the death of
Solomon, have never returned to their former glory.

H. G. Wells, in his classic historical saga, *The
Outline of History*, said, "In 745 BC arose another
Tiglath Pileser, Tiglath Pileser III, the Tiglath Pilser
of the Bible (II Kings xv, 29, and xvi, 7 *et seq.*). He
not only directed the transfer of the Israelites to
Media (the 'Ten Lost Tribes' whose ultimate fate
has exercised so many curious minds), but he
conquered and ruled Babylon, so founding what
historians know as the New Assyrian Empire."[4]

The prophet Jeremiah was born about 640 BC, in
Anathoth, just north of Jerusalem. As a youth, he
felt called, wanting to unite Israel under Yahweh.
When Nebuchadnezzar invaded Palestine in 604, he
reduced King Jehoiakim to the status of a vassal. In
597, he invaded Jerusalem and assassinated the
king, making his eighteen-year-old son, Jehoiachin,
heir. He reigned mere months before surrendering.[5]

When Zedekiah led Judah into rebellion against
Babylon, the prophet Jeremiah, who had predicted
that this action would bring disaster, was considered
a traitor. In July 587, the Babylonians destroyed
Jerusalem, stripping the Temple of its valuables.[6]

After the Assyrian Conquest, the "Lost Tribes of Israel" were exiled. More than one belief exists as to their identity.

There is one widely believed theory, held by the Church of Jesus Christ of Latter Day Saints, which proclaims the *original* inhabitants of the Americas as being descendants of the Lost Tribes of Israel, according to the **Book of Mormon**.

There are others, including some proposed by current authors, Gary David (as shared within **Eye of the Phoenix**, also being published in 2008) being but one, that denote pre-Columbian travel as having come from not only the Far East, but also quite likely from the Middle East, Egypt and Europe.[7] It has been through comparative linguistics and religious beliefs of the early indigenous peoples of the Western Hemisphere, that this has since come to be known.

An earlier brilliant author, Rutgers University Professor, Ivan Van Sertima, presented a striking case for ancient Egyptian travel to the West in **They Came Before Columbus**, as published by **Random House** in 1976.

The most widely accepted theory, however, aside from those believing that the so called "lost tribes" are not really lost, but were dissolved into the worldwide Jewish population, is accepted by numerous groups today.

Although this argument is several centuries old, it has only been over the past 150 years that individuals have begun identifying themselves as proponents of "British Israelism", a belief that is synonymous with the fact that the throne of David is currently occupied by the Queen of England, and that the royal houses of Europe are descended from the lineage of King David.

In keeping, the nation of England is viewed as modern Ephraim, the United States as Manasseh, Denmark or Danmark as Dan's mark, and together with Sweden, or Swe DAN, the Tribe of Dan, and so forth. The Danube River and Danzig are viewed as other clues. France is seen by many lost tribe writers as being Reuben in biblical prophecy. It needs to be further noted that *Berith* is the Hebrew word for covenant, and *Ish* is the Hebrew word for man. In combining these two words, the word *Berith-ish* meaning "Covenant Man" is believed to form the basis for the word British.[8]

An early modern advocate of British Israelism, as mentioned in chapter one, was the controversial Iowa-born[9], California-based minister, Herbert W. Armstrong (1892-1986), the founder of an international church called *The Worldwide Church of God*. His radio and TV broadcast, **The World Tomorrow**, was beamed around the globe. One of his most popular books was ***The United States and the British Commonwealth in Prophecy***. Much of what is taught today by proponents of these beliefs can be traced to this remarkably high-quality work.

Armstrong met, at intervals, with many world leaders. He would send out, free of charge to anyone, copies of the books he wrote, including his *Plain Truth Magazine*. Another outreach was Ambassador College in Pasadena, and its satellite in Big Sandy, Texas, of which he was the founder. Though his organization was divided following his death, Armstrong is believed by some groups today to have been a prophet.

One living advocate of these same teachings is Yair Davidiy, a Jewish scholar who heads an organization known as "Brit-Am", centered in Jerusalem. Davidiy has written a book on the subject called *The Tribes*. Parts of this book can be found in video format as posted on the YouTube website.

In a personal email, Davidiy quoted from the first chapter of his book, pointing out the fact that the Bible says that "The King of Assyria took Sameria, and carried Israel away into Assyria, and placed them in Hala, and in Habor, and in the cities of the Medes" (II Kings 17:6). Davidiy further states, "The Bible also mentions 'Hara' (I Chronicles 5:26) in Eastern Iran as a place of exile. In keeping, both archaeological findings and they have enabled the identification of these places of re-settlement."

According to Davidiy, shortly after both exile and re-settlement, every one of the said places became a center for a group of peoples who then appeared for the first time. They are known to history as the

"Cimmerians, Sythians, and Guti, or Goths." His book brings out detailed and compelling arguments that these entities were, at least, part of the Ten Lost Tribes of Israel.

Dividiy states most emphatically, on his website, that "Reuben became prominent amongst the French who were dominated by the Ribuari and Rubi Franks and other groups named after clans of Reuben."[10] He further points out that the sons of Asher were Jimnah, and Ishuah, and Isui, and Beriah, correspond to the tribes of the Lygian Goths. According to him, "Jimnah became the Omani, Isui the Heissi, and Beriah the Boreoi." [11]

Beginning in Genesis 48:14, we find yet another clue as to the identity of the descendants of Israel, proclaimed by British Israelism.

Due to Joseph's special gifts, he was granted an exalted position in Egypt, a position which came to be the salvation of Israel in time of great famine. Israel (formerly known as Jacob) blessed the children of Joseph in a special way.

The laying on of the right hand, in a blessing that was reserved for the firstborn, denoted receipt of the greater portion of inheritance. Israel stretched out his right hand; he laid it upon Ephraim's head, the younger, thereby placing his left hand upon Manasseh's head, the firstborn.

And he blessed Joseph and said, "God, before whom my fathers Abraham and Isaac did walk, the God which fed me all my life long unto this day, The Angel which redeemed me from evil, bless the lads; **and let my name be named on them (Israel).** And the name of my fathers, Abraham and Isaac; and let them grow into a multitude in the midst of the earth. And when Joseph saw that his father had his right hand upon the head of Ephraim, it displeased him; and he held up his father's hand, to remove it from Ephraim's head unto Manasseh's head. And Joseph said unto his father, Not so, my father; for this is the firstborn; put thy right hand upon his head. And his father refused, and said, I know *it* my son, I know *it*; he also shall become a people, and he also shall be great; but truly his younger brother shall become **a multitude of nations**". (Genesis 48:15-19)

According to the teachings of British Israelism, **Israel's name was to be upon the descendants of Joseph**. These were divided into two half tribes, Ephraim and Manasseh, after the two sons to whom Israel gave special blessings. They were among the Lost Tribes dispersed into the world. The youngest was to become a multitude, or company, of nations; this is attributed to The British Commonwealth. The other, would be closely related, and be a great nation. This, it is said, is the United States.

In *The Outline of History*, from which I quoted earlier, H.G. Wells later stated, "In our accounts of the development of the Western world we have had occasion to name the Scythians, and to explain the difficulty of distinguishing clearly between Cimmerians, Sarmatians, Medes, Persians, Partheans, Goths, and other more or less nomadic, more or less Ayran peoples who drifted to and fro in a great arc between the Danube and central Asia." [12]

After that, Wells wrote, "The populations of South Scotland, England, East Ireland, Flanders, Normandy, and the Russias have more elements in common than we are accustomed to recognize. All are fundamentally Goths and Nordic peoples." [13]

The Hebrides Islands in Scotland are said to be derived from the word Hebrew. [14]

The Stone of Scone is reported to have been taken to Scotia by Jeremiah the Prophet (often identified as Ollam Fodhla), who felt compelled to transport Teia Tephi, the princess of Israel, there after the dispersion, thereby preserving the throne of Israel. According to the legend, she married Eochaidh, the High King of Ireland. Princess Tephi was mentioned by Armstrong in his compelling, though mostly undocumented, book, *The United States and British Commonwealth in Prophecy*, as early as the 1950's (several editions were published).

The stone is said to have remained in Scotia, used as a base upon which kings were crowned. King Edward I took the stone, or, according to some reports, a fake stone, from Scotland to England in 1296, placing it beneath the Coronation Chair in

Westminster Abbey, where it reportedly remained, becoming the Coronation Stone for the kings of England for centuries.[15] Branches of British Israelism are today headquartered in the US, Canada, and the UK.

The Phoenicians were a Canaanite tribe. Homer called them the Sidonians. Their cities lay along the Mediterranean coast, west of Lebanon, except for Dor, north of Mount Carmel. The most important cities, mentioned in the *el-Amarna letters*, were Acco, Tyre (*Sor*, "the rock"), Sidon, Beiruit, Byblos (Gebal), Symira, Arward, and Ugarit (Ras Shamra). The language of the Phoenicians was one of the western Semetic dialects, closely akin to Hebrew.[16] The Hebrews were greatly influenced by the Phoenicians. El, a common name for God, utilized in many Hebrew names, was taken from them. According to Judges, chapter eighteen, the tribe of Dan took over the city of Laish, north of Israel near the Phoenicians, and re-named it "Dan". The fact that the Phoenicians were sea-faring people is well documented by historians.

It is believed by **The Hope of Israel Ministries**, among others, that: "Dan, who 'abode in ships,' made common concourse with the Phoenicians, intermarried with them, and established colonies throughout the Mediterranean region". It is further stated by these researchers that "As the Israelites migrated through Europe, they fulfilled this prophecy (Dan was to be 'a serpent by the way'), and left 'ROAD SIGNS' and 'GUIDEPOSTS' along the way, so that we can trace their route!" [17]

The chief tribe to do this was Dan, because of their proclivity to leave the name of their ancestor "DAN" everywhere they went. This prophecy was also mentioned by Armstrong in *The United States and British Commonwealth in Prophecy*,[18] and every researcher on the prophetic aspects of the Tribe of Dan, no matter what the teaching, agrees that they are very important in both history and prophecy.

In Hebrew there are no vowels, so the name Dan is written DN, or its Hebrew equivalent. Thus words like Dan, Din, Don, Dun, Den, or Dn, correspond to the name of Dan.

The ancient Irish history known as *the Annals of the Four Masters* (*Annala na gCeithre Mháistrí*), is housed in the Royal Academy in Dublin. This text states that they are records from the beginning of Irish history, from the year 2242 after creation to 1616 AD.

One of the annals documents the reign of Eochaidh, son of Erc, (who seems to be this king) and tells of the invasion of the Tuatha De Dananns,[19] whom many see as the Tribe of Dan. There is also an ancient legend that they were a divine tribe. The only mention of the wife of Eochaidh says simply: "Taillte, daughter of Maghmor, King of Spain, and the wife of Eochaidh".[20]

In their current form, which was compiled from earlier manuscripts, they were written between January 1632 and August 1636 in a Franciscan monastery in County Donegal. There are, however, debates as to when the original records were compiled. Claiming to be the history of Ireland from just prior to the flood, the earliest entries are thought to have actually been compiled no earlier than 550 AD.[21]

It is quite possible that they were either passed down verbally, or like many other ancient texts, copied from earlier manuscripts no longer in existence. Given these factors, it has been impossible to determine, with any plausible degree of certainty, if there was, indeed, an Israelite princess who was married to Eochaidh.

The Christian Assemblies International website reports that there are sceptics who claim that "Tea-Tephi never existed and was a made-up character. The British Israel World Federation even now admits that she never existed. She was an invention of a British-Israel expositor named F.R.A. Glover in 1861 and the myth was perpetuated unchecked."

This site, in answer to a question asked them concerning this subject, also posted the following: "The BIWF, however, firmly asserts that one of the royal daughters mentioned in the book of Jeremiah WAS INDEED MARRIED TO A JUDAHTE and indeed contributed to the upholding of the royal, Davidic line. We have contacted Michael Clark, the

Deputy President of the BIWF in London, in person, and he has given us permission to CLARIFY THE MISCONCEPTION that the BIWF had abandoned the idea of a royal princess moving to Ireland (some people had erroneously thought so)."

There still seems to be no limit to the number of books promoting the Tea Tephi character.

Not everyone who advances this teaching, however, is as credible as those mentioned previously. One such example is a modern self-proclaimed advocate of "The Long Awaited Truth of All Things on Planet Earth", whose real name is A.J. Hill, though he goes by the symbolic title, "Jah".

Hill claims to have uncovered the autobiography of "Princess Teia Tephi".[22] The book chronicles the fall of Jerusalem, her subsequent journey to Ireland, with the Lia Fail (Stone of Destiny), and the Ark of the Covenant., via Tanis in Egypt (as in "Raiders of The Lost Ark") then on to Gibraltar (where it is recorded that she was proclaimed queen of the "Gadite Israelites", the descendants of Gad, son of Judah, who lived there); Breogan in Spain; Cornwall and eventually landing at Howth, near Dublin on the 18th of June 583 BC.

The following parallel is drawn between the prophecy in the Book of Jeremiah and the writing attributed to Teia Tephi, also claimed to be written in the sixth century BC.

Jeremiah 1:10
*See, I have this day set thee over the nations and over the kingdoms, to **ROOT** out, and to pull down, and to **DESTROY**, and to throw down, to build and to **PLANT**.*

In The Book of Tephi, there are a number of quotations that relate strongly to the Bible.

For example, Teia Tephi expands on what Jeremiah wrote in The Bible in this excerpt:

Book of Tephi 2:2
*Tephi, I was but weak, a little thing in men's eyes, A tender twig of the Cedar, yet sheltered of prophecies. The Prophet of God revealed this. Is not his speech made plain? He came to "**ROOT** and **DESTROY**". He went forth "to **PLANT** again".*

The book goes on to relate significant events which have taken place in later history, along with some curious predictions which have not yet been fulfilled, including a prophecy that she would be recovered from her tomb on the "Hill of Tara" in County Meath, Ireland, along with the fabled Ark of the Covenant.

For those wishing to check out Hill's website, go to http://jahtruth.net/ for more information.

Jah is a name used for God, a short form of Yahweh, or Jehovah. Hill, a British native who claims to have a military background, wrote a book first printed in 1986 in Spain titled *The Way Home or Face the Fire, The Survival Plan for all Human+ Beings*, in which he identifies himself as the prophesied returned Christ / Prince Michael.[23] Also promoted on the site is the Koran.

The *Book of Teia Tephi* is sanctioned as genuine on the web site **The Seventh Fire**[24], a site promoting spiritualism. Likewise for a site titled **Revelations of the Bible**[25], which publicizes Davidic genealogical lines, the ideals of Herbert W. Armstrong, mysteries and hidden knowledge.

The flag of Ulster, now Northern Ireland, features a red hand on a Star of David, situated in the center, atop a red cross on a white background, clear symbols of Israel's royalty. Israel's son, Judah, had twin sons, Zarah and Pharez. Genesis 38: 28-30 tells the following story:

28. "As she was giving birth, one of them put out his hand; so the midwife took a scarlet thread and tied it on his wrist and said, "This one came out first."

29. But when he drew back his hand, his brother came out, and she said, "So this is how you have broken out!" And he was named Perez.

30. Then his brother, who had the scarlet thread on his wrist, came out and he was given the name Zerah. (NIV)

It is told that Zerah became known as "Zerah of the Red Hand", and went into exile in Iberia, or Heberia, the land of the Hebrew. He is said to have been the builder of Zaragossa (stronghold of Zerah). Later when Babylon, then Rome, invaded Iberia (Spain), they drove the descendants of Zerah northward to Galacia and Viscaya (Biscay), and many sailed to Hibernia, the new land of the Hebrews, now Ireland. [26]

While these theories seem to hold some merit from a historical prospective, it is becoming quite clear from the proof of DNA that not all persons of Western European ancestry are descended through direct male lines from the ancient Israelites. Since many haplogroups are represented in the UK alone, in order to determine one's specific ancestry, it is necessary to obtain genealogical DNA testing.

I have written an article titled, *"Genealogy by Genetics, Why Test"*, which may be found in its entirety on the St. Clair Research web site at http://www.stclairresearch.com, that has since been published in the official Clan Sinclair publications in the US, Canada, the UK and Australia. Briefly stated, Y-DNA testing of male chromosomes traces common ancestry of direct male lineage using a set of markers known as alleles. Mutation occurs for various reasons, including viruses caught by ancestors. Feelings on the rate of mutation vary, and it is the belief of Steve St. Clair, head of the Sinclair/St. Clair DNA Project, and me, as his co-founder and partner, that this rate is not entirely consistent in various lines. To show direct maternal origins, mitochondrial DNA may also be tested.

Data on how haplogroups determine ancestry may be found at the site. Our study suggests, as do others, that the majority of Caucasoid Western Europeans and natives of the British Isles are of the R1b haplogroup, and have been in Europe since the last Ice Age, estimated to be 10,000 years ago.

Jewish males generally belong to haplogroup E3b, into which one member of our project fits; and Cohens, said to be descendants of Moses' brother, Aaron, of the tribe of Levi, are haplogroup J.

E3b, however, may not have been around from the beginning of the history of Israel. The Bene Israel, a Jewish community in Western India, with traditions of Jewish descent, has a high frequency of the Cohen Modal Haplotype J, further substantiating these claims. While they lack haplogroup E3b, the authors of the linked study suggest that they split from other Jews before E3b entered the Jewish gene pool.[27] Also, some have shown to be Q, a type is found in a large area from Norway to Iran, as well as Mongolia, and the Americas.

According to one web site, the R1b haplogroup is found in a small percentage of Ashkenazi Jews (roughly 10%).[28] Whether they descended from the Turkish-Mongol mixed people known as Khazars of the seventh to tenth century, who converted to their national religion of Judaism, is highly debated. One theory even sees most modern Jews of these lines.[29]

Chapter 11 Footnotes

[1]TMC Entertainment. (2005). *Walking the Bible Timeline – A Journey By Land Through The Five Books by Moses*. Retrieved March 2008 at http://www.pbs.org/walkingthebible/timeline.html
[2]Seiglie, Mario. (1997). *Archaeology and the Book of Joshua: The Conquest*. Retrieved March 2008 from http://www.ucgstp.org/lit/gn/gn011/archaeol.html
[3]Maspero, G. *History of Egypt*. Volume VII, Part B. Retrieved March 2008 from http://www.gutenberg.org/files/17327/17327-h/v7b.htm
[4]Wells, H.G. (1949). *The Outline of History, Being a Plain History of Life and Mankind, Volume 1* (p 168). Doubleday and Co.: Garden City, NY.
[5]Lockyer, Herbert, Sr. (Ed.) (1986). Dipsersion of the Jewish People (p. 306). *The Liberty Illustrated Bible Dictionary*. Thomas Nelson Publishers: Nashville, TN.
[6]St. Clair, Stanley J. (2006). *Prayers of Prophets, Knights and Kings* (p 25). Trafford Publishing Co.: Victoria, BC.
[7]David, Gary A. *Votan: Diffusionist Deity*. Retrieved March 2008 from http://www.viewzone.com/votan.html
[8]Hand, Gary A. *British Israelism: Religious and Pseudo-historical belief*. Retrieved March 2008 from http://www.ondoctrine.com/10brtish.htm
[9]Brace, Robin A. (2006). *A Concise Look at the Founder of the Worldwide Church of God, Herbert W. Armstrong. Where Did He Come From? What Did He Believe?* Retrieved March 2008 from

http://www.ukapologetics.net/1bioherb.html

[10]Davidiy, Yair. *The Tribe of Ruben*. Retrieved March 2008 from
http://www.britam.org/reuben.html

[11]Davidiy, Yair. *The Israelite Tribe of Asher*. Retrieved March 2008 from
http://www.britam.org/asher.html

[12]Wells, H.G. (1949). *The Outline of History, Being a Plain History of Life and Mankind, Volume 1* (p 504). Doubleday and Co.: Garden City, NY.

[13]Ibid. Volume II, p 663

[14]St. Clair, Stanley J. (2006). *Prayers of Prophets, Knights and Kings* (pp 71-72). Trafford Publishing Co.: Victoria, BC.

[15]Ibid p 40

[16]Langer, William L. (1940). *The Encyclopedia of World History* (p 32). Houghton Mifflin Co.: New York, NY.

[17]Dankenbring, William F. and Keyser, John D. *The Serpent's Trail - The Mysterious Tribe of Dan*. Retrieved March 2008 from
http://www.hope-of-israel.org/i000035a.htm

[18]Armstrong, Herbert W. (1967). *The United States and British Commonwealth in Prophecy* (pp 126-128). Ambassador College Press: Pasadena, CA.

[19]*Annals of the Four Masters*. Annal M3303.1 (click on M3274 and scroll down to M3303.1 at the very bottom) Retrieved March 2008 from
http://www.ucc.ie/celt/online/T100005A/

[20]Ibid, Annal M3304 (scroll down to M3370.2)

[21]Sewell, Robert. (2006). *Ireland - Early Irish History*. Retrieved March 2008 from
http://www.robertsewell.ca/ireland.html

[22]Jah. *The Book of Tephi, Queen of Tara and Gibralter*. Retrieved March 2008 from http://jahtruth.net/tephi.htm

[23]Hill, A. J. (1986). *The Way Home or Face the Fire, The Survival Plan for all Human+Beings* (p 123). JAH Publications: San Roque, Spain.

[24]The7thfire.com. (2007). *The Seventh Fire*. Retrieved March 2008 from http://www.the7thfire.com/index2.htm

[25]*Revelations of the Bible – Teia Tephi*. Retrieved March 2008 from http://www.revelationsofthebible.com/Tea.htm

[26]The7thfire.com. (2007). *The True Origin of the Ulster Flag*. Retrieved March 2008 from http://www.the7thfire.com/queen_tephi/flag_of_ Ulster.html

[27]*Dienekes' Anthropology Blog: Haplotype E3b and Ancient Jews*. Retrieved March 2008 from http://dienekes.blogspot.com/2004/12/haplogroup-e3b-and-ancient-jews.html

[28]Jewish Ethnicity – Haplogroup R1b Yahoo Group. Retrieved March 2008 from http://groups.yahoo.com/group/JewishR1b/

[29] Glogoczowski, Marek. (2005) *Most Jews Are Not Semites.* Retrieved April 2006 from http://www.rense.com/general66/mostjewsare not.htm

Chapter Twelve
The Magi

A number of explanations have been attempted through the Christian era to identify the wise men that are recorded as having traveled from the east to find the new born king of the Jews. Their story is introduced to us in the second chapter of the Gospel attributed to Matthew. This account tells us that they first came to Jerusalem "Saying, Where is he that has been born King of the Jews? For we have seen his star in the east, and are come to worship him"(v2).

The story relates that word reached Herod, the puppet ruler of Judea under the Romans, and he was "troubled, and all Jerusalem with him" (v3). Expectations of a messiah were not uncommon, so he summoned his priests and scribes to find out where it had been prophesied that he should be born (v4). "And they said unto him, In Bethlehem of Judea: for it is written by the prophet" (v5). After this, Herod called for an audience with the wise men, asking them when the star had appeared. He then sent them to Bethlehem, asking of them to find the child, and bring him word, so he could "come and worship him also" (v8). The wise men left, and found that the star "went before them till it came and stood over where the young child was" (v9). They entered and "fell down, and worshiped him: and when they had opened their treasures, they presented him gifts; gold, frankincense, and myrrh" (v11).

Following this meeting, it is recorded that they were "warned of God in a dream that they should not return to Herod" (v12), journeying home on a different route.

The account from Matthew also tells us that Joseph had a dream in which an angel appeared to him, telling him to take Mary and the "young child", Jesus, and "flee into Egypt, and be thou there until I bring thee word: for Herod will seek the young child to destroy him" (v13).

Herod, it is written, upon realizing that the wise men were not coming back, was very angry. He immediately ordered that "all children that were in Bethlehem, and all the coasts thereof, from two years old and under", be killed (v16).

Who were these "wise men", commonly called Magi? Did such a "star" appear around the time of the birth of Jesus?

The teaching that there were three of these eastern visitors is traditional and quite likely derived from the number of gifts which were presented to the Christ Child. Tradition as established in the seventh century claims their names to have been Casper, Melchoir, and Belthasar.

The Greek word *magos,* μάγο, comes from the ancient Persian Aryan "Magupat". This term is a specific occupational title referring to the priestly caste of a distorted form of Zoroastrianism, known as Zurvanism[1]. As a part of their religious practice, they were highly tuned to the stars, thereby gaining an international reputation as astronomers.

The similarities of Zoroastrianism to Judaism are strong, and may stem from the time of Queen Esther in the fifth century BC, when Zoroastrianism was beginning to take root. It is at this time that the Jews were under Persian authority, following the Babylonian captivity with the overthrow of Babylon by the Persians in 557 BC.

As an influential group, the Magi were advisors to the kings. They believed in a prophecy that God was going to send a messiah, meaning an anointed one.

There are at least two possibilities as to the identity of the star, which these Magi are recorded to have followed. Given the fact that Herod the Great reigned from 8 to 4 BC, we know that the true birth date of Jesus, based on the scriptural account of Matthew, would have been within those years.

According to a BBC television special, on April 16, 6 BC, Jupiter was in the eastern sky, eclipsed with the moon. Michael Molnar of Rutgers University discovered a coin dating to around the time of Jesus' birth, depicting Aries, the Ram, jumping, looking back at a star. This clue led to documents showing that Judea was often depicted under the sign of Aries. To the Magi, this could have been a sign of the birth of the messiah.

There exists another, even more likely, possibility. The most probable time, in my opinion, for Mary's conception can be found in the first chapter of the Gospel of Luke, verse twenty-six and twenty-seven:

"And in the sixth month the angel Gabriel was sent from God unto a city of Galilee named Nazareth, To a virgin espoused to a man whose name was Joseph, of the house of David, and the virgin's name was Mary."

Although this could have related to the sixth month of Elizabeth's pregnancy with John, as some feel, it is more likely to have been the sixth month of the Hebrew religious calendar, which was the month of Ada, from the Akkadian *Adaru*, (February/March). Given the office and duties of John the Baptist's father, Zachariah, the timing of the angel Gabriel's visit to Mary, and the reign of Herod, a very realistic birth date for the Christ Child would have been mid Tishri, or early October, 7 BC.[2]

In 1603, Dutch astronomer and mathematician Johannes Kepler became the first to observe a conjunction between the planets Jupiter and Saturn in the Constellation Pisces, noting that by their converging, they appeared as a larger and new "star"[3]. Later, Kepler remembered having read the writings of Isaac Abravanel[4], a brilliant Portuguese rabbi who lived from 1436-1508, in which he stated that Jewish astronomers believed that when there was a conjunction of Jupiter and Saturn in Pisces, the messiah would come.

This hypothesis was reexamined in 1925, when references to this conjunction were discovered in the cuneiform inscriptions of the archives of the ancient Babylonian School of Astrology at Sippar.

This conjunction had been recorded over a period of five months in 7 BC. Calculations show that this bright "star" became visible three times over the course of that year: May 29th, **October3** [rd], and December 4th. [5] The Persian Magi would have been aware of this.

Given Mary's probable date of conception, the October date of birth would have been slightly premature, but with the journey to Bethlehem on a donkey, this makes considerable sense.

Chapter 12 Footnotes

[1]*Magi* retrieved from Wikipedia, the free encyclopedia website located at http://en.wikipedia.org/wiki/Magi
[2]Warren, Tony. (1998). *Can We Know What Year Jesus Was Born?*Retrieved March 2008 from http://www.mountainretreatorg.net/faq/birth.html
[3]*Possible Explanations for the Star of Bethlehem* Retrieved February 2008 from http://www.astrosurf.com/comets/cometas/Star/Possible.html
[4]Kayserling, Meyer and Ginzberg, Louis. *Abravanel*. Retrieved March 2008 from JewishEncyclopedia.com located at http://www.jewishencyclopedia.com/view.jsp?artid=631&letter=A
[5]Kilmon, Jack. *History and the New Testament*. Retieved March 2008 from http://www.historian.net/NTHX.html

Adoration of the Magi
by Ernest Bradfield Freed

Chapter Thirteen
Mary Magdalene

Mary of Magdala has been the object of speculation and wonder for all of Christendom since early in the church age. The Catholic Church taught, for centuries, that she was a prostitute before she began to follow Jesus. This idea originated in the sixth century, when Pope Gregory I identified her as both the woman spoken of in Luke 7:37, and the woman who washed Jesus' feet with her hair.[1]

In scripture, she is identified as one out of whom seven demons were cast.[2] Some groups today see her as a goddess.[3] She is claimed, in an alarming number of modern books, including *The Da Vinci Code*, to have been the wife of Jesus.

Like so many, she was identified by her native home, Magdala, seen in Christian circles as a town on the southwest coast of the Sea of Galilee. It is not a matter of debate that after Jesus delivered her from her demons, she became one of his closest followers.

Some see her as the woman caught in adultery, recorded in John 8:1-11, although there is no evidence for this, scripturally or otherwise, while others identify her as having been Mary of Bethany, the sister of Martha and Lazarus. Arguments for this are wholly speculative.

In *The God-Kings of Europe*, the first in the "God-King" series, British professor Hugh Montgomery claims that Jesus was married to both Mary of Magdala and Mary of Bethany, an idea deemed so radical that no other writer, of whom I am familiar, has ever dared to proclaim such a thing.

There is no doubt that Mary felt a special connection to Jesus. She supported his ministry, was at his crucifixion, and is recorded as being the first to witness his resurrection.[4] If Jesus was married, as suggested by several writers, most notably in *Holy Blood, Holy Grail* and *The Da Vinci Code*, but including the many other books and articles which they, in turn, have sparked, Mary Magdalene would seem to have been the most logical candidate. This is a teaching that has been rejected by most Christians; and one which has given me a great deal of struggle.

It seemed that the first hint of this idea came from a Frenchman by the name of Pierre Plantard. He also claimed that a secret society named the **Priory of Sion** had been in existence in Europe since the Middle Ages. It was said that its members were the keepers of a dark secret that would turn the Christian world upside down. Plantard claimed that the Grand Masters of this organization, one of which had been Leonardo Da Vinci, were the protectors of a royal bloodline which sprang from Jesus and Mary Magdalene, one that has been ruling Europe for thousands of years.

The dubious basis of this tale stated that Jesus, having been fully human, had not died on the cross, and that, as the true heir to the throne of David, he had preserved this bloodline through his child, or children, by Mary Magdalene, his wife.

Following the crucifixion, in which either someone took his place, or he was taken down from the cross while still alive, he hid from his enemies. Mary and their child, or children, escaped to France with Joseph of Arimathea, said to have been the uncle of Mary, the mother of Jesus (see next chapter). This is the story that was originally published in England (1982) by Michael Baigent, Richard Leigh, and Henry Lincoln as *The Holy Blood and the Holy Grail*. Later released in the US as *Holy Blood, Holy Grail*, the book was not highly publicized, and resultantly was not taken seriously by most Americans.

Pierre Plantard was later exposed as a fraud. The Priory of Sion, which had been a real organization in the Middle Ages, soon ceased to exist. *The Secret Dossiers*, which the authors found in the library in Paris, was, admittedly, a forgery.

But that is by no means the whole story, for this idea did not begin with Lincoln, Leigh, and Baigent, or even with Plantard.

In 1906, a stained glass window produced by Stephen Adam was placed in the Kilmore Church in Dervaig, the Scottish western Isle of Mull, depicting

Jesus, with a halo, holding hands with a young lady with no halo, appearing heavily pregnant. Below the picture, the words read, "Mary hath chosen that good part which shall not be taken away from her". This is a direct quote from the words of Jesus in Luke 10:42, directed to Martha of Bethany in regard to her sister Mary's choice to remain close to him while she was anxious over household duties. In Gaelic, Kilmore is Caell Meire, which means, "Church of Mary" This is only one reason to consider the teaching that Mary of Bethany and Mary Magdalene were the same individual.

As early as 1946, a novel by Robert Graves, *King Jesus,* suggested that Jesus was married to Mary Magdalene, and that their lineage was concealed from all but the royalist elite, in order to protect the royal bloodline.[5]

According to the Gnostic *Gospel of Phillip*, "the companion of the [   ] Mary Magdalene, [   ] her more [   ] the disciples [   ] kiss her [   ] on her [   ]." In each bracketed spot, a hole in the parchment only allows readers to speculate, but from the rest of the text, there is no doubt that Jesus is the person being discussed. Although there is no mention, even here, of marriage, proponents state that the word translated as "companion" in this context is a word which was used for spouse. The debate that continues to rage is whether the original language was Syriac or Greek, with opponents noting that the Gnostic Gospels date to the third century AD.

Several authors, in writing about the historical Jesus, have denoted that, as a Rabbi, it would have been mandatory for him to have been married. Another argument used is that the wedding in Cana, in which Jesus preformed his first miracle, turning water into wine, was the marriage of Jesus himself. His mother directed the servants regarding Jesus, "Whatsoever he sayeth unto you, do it".[6] It is quite obvious here that Mary, the mother of Jesus, is in a role of leadership, possibly even hostess, of the wedding.

Following the publication of **Holy Blood, Holy Grail**, there are some Christian theologians, such as Margaret Starbird, who have come to believe, following a thorough examination of the Gospels, coupled with non-canonical writings, such as the **Gospel of Mary,** and the **Gospel of Phillip**, that Jesus was indeed married, resulting in a sacred bloodline. A few have expressed that even a divine Jesus could have married.

Pertinent books by Starbird include **The Woman with the Alabaster Jar, The Goddess of the Gospels**, and **Magdalene's Lost Legacy**. Ms. Starbird sees the name given to Mary's native home as being a reference to Magdaleder, found in the Book of Micah, "the promise of the restoration of Sion following her exile." She points out that the place name Magdal-eder literally means "tower of the flock" in the same sense as a high place used by a shepherd from which to watch the sheep.[7]

While there are other authors who have also capitalized on this story, seemingly placing a number of other pieces in the puzzle, much too numerous to be covered adequately in this text, it needs to be shared that this theory is now widely believed and accepted around the world.

Regardless of differing opinions as to whether Jesus was married, there has been an alarming amount of evidence that the Merovingian Dynasty, said to have descended from Jesus and Mary Magdalene, has living descendants today.

Early in the third century (200's AD), Christian historian Julius Africanus identified a group of families who went about as traveling preachers labeled as the *Desposynoi*, Greek for "The Master's People". From the Galilean villages of Nazareth and Kokhaba, they availed of genealogies and are said to have been the descendants of James, brother of Jesus, who was the leader of the early church in Jerusalem, and other members of Jesus' family.[8] "The Lord's brothers" were cited by St. Paul as being disciples who took their wives on trips with them.[9]

"James the Just" was succeeded by his brother, Simon, as church leader, and some family members are believed to have been part of the Diaspora of the first century.[10]

My article, *The Nose Knows, The Hallmark of the Merovingians?* published in the UK in *The Temple Booklet Issue No. 12*, March 31, 2008, explores physical similarities in those claiming to be the progeny of this dynasty. [11]

Those identified as descendants of the Merovingian lines include the Stewarts and other British royal families. There is wide-spread anticipation that they will, one day, openly identify themselves as the heirs to the Davidic throne, and become the great dominators of world politics - or are they already?

Chapter 13 Footnotes

[1]B&L Publications (2007). *Jesus and Mary Magdalene: Did they have a secret marriage?* Retrieved March 2008 from Y-Jesus Magazine located at http://y- jesus.com/jesus_married. php?gclid=CL76u9ez-JACFQTslgod7zze1Q

[2]Luke 8:2, Mark 26:9

[3]Starbird, Margaret. (1998). *The Goddess in the Gospels*. Bear & Co.: Rochester, VT.

[4]Mark 26:9

[5]Starbird, Margaret. (1993). *The Woman with the Alabaster Jar* excerpt located at http://www.beliefnet.com/story/134/story_13494_1. html (Retrieved January 2008)

[6]John 4:5

[7]Starbird, Margaret. (1993). *The Woman with the Alabaster Jar* excerpt located at http://www.beliefnet.com/story/134/story_13494_1. html (Retrieved January 2008)

[8]*The Genealogy of Jesus, Part Five*. Retrieved March 2008 from http://www.pursiful.com/chronology/gen_jesus5. html

[9]I Corinthians 9:5, TLB

[10]*Jewish Virtual Library - The Diaspora*. Retrieved March 2008 from American-Israeli Cooperative Enterprise website located at http://www.jewishvirtuallibrary.org/jsource/History/ Diaspora.html

[11]St. Clair, Stan (2008) *The Nose Knows, The Hallmark of the Merovingians? Temple Booklet* Issue No. *12*, Wells, Somerset, UK

Chapter Fourteen
Joseph of Arimathea

Joseph of Arimathea, a wealthy follower of Jesus, appears in Christian scriptures only after the crucifixion, when he asks Pilate for the privilege of taking down Jesus' body from the cross. Arimathea was said to be a "City of Judea". Some scholars have thought it to be the same as Ramathiam in Ephraim, the recorded birthplace of the prophet Samuel (I Samuel 1:1 and 19), while others think that it may be the same as Ramleh in Dan, or perhaps Rama in Benjamin.[1]

Mentioned in all four Gospels, his story is recorded in the Gospel attributed to Matthew, 27:57-60. In the Gospel of Mark, chapter fifteen, verse forty-three, he is referred to as "an honorable counsellor which also waited for the kingdom of God." In Luke's Gospel, chapter twenty-three, verse fifty-one, he is spoken of as "a good man, and a just". Finally, in the Gospel attributed to the Apostle John, 19:38, he is said to be a disciple of Jesus, albeit "secretly".

It is according to the Matthew account that he was granted Jesus' body, whereby he "wrapped it in a clean linen cloth, and laid it in his own new tomb, which he had hewn out in the rock; and rolled a great stone to the door of the sepulcher, and departed."

In Greek, Luke calls him a *bouleutes,* literally "a senator". As a result, biblical scholars agree that Joseph was a member of the Sanhedrin, the Jewish legal council which condemned Jesus. It is stated in verse fifty-one that he "had not consented to the council and deed of them", so he may have been absent at the trial.

According to the John account, Nicodemus, also a wealthy member of the Sanhedrin, and secret follower of Jesus, brought spices for the anointing of the body.

Nowhere else is Joseph mentioned in canonical scripture, nor are we told that he had any relationship to Mary or Jesus. However, tales of him are related in non-canonical books such as of *The Acts of Pilate*, in medieval days being more commonly referred to as *The Gospel of Nicodemus* due to its authorship being incorrectly attributed to him, and *The Narrative of Joseph of Arimathea*, proclaiming in the opening greeting to be written by him. This particular book, with but five chapters, largely deals with the glorification of the robber, therein called "Demas", to whom Jesus promises, while on the cross, that he shall be with him in paradise. A third Apocryphal source is called *The Passing of Mary*, in which Joseph is identified as the author only at its very conclusion.

Though a minor character in the canon, and even in the Apocryphal writings of the second century, medieval legend claims that the Apostle Phillip,

Lazarus, Mary Magdalene, and others, went on an evangelical mission to Gaul in either 63 AD or 37 AD, alternatively. [2] These legends further state that Mary remained at Marseilles while others, including Joseph, traveled northward to establish Christianity in Britain, the most remote corner of the Roman Empire. It has been claimed that Joseph, having become wealthy in the trade of metals, was likely acquainted with the isle of Britain.

As mentioned earlier, there exists a common teaching that Joseph of Arimathea was an uncle to Mary, and thus a great-uncle to Jesus. Some have felt that Jesus, as a lad, may well have traveled to Britain with him on business. In response to this belief, William Blake's famous hymn, *Jerusalem* (1804), cries out, "And did those feet in ancient times, walk upon England's mountains green?"

It has also been claimed that Joseph went first to Glastonbury. A popular story, told here, has Joseph bringing a staff, grown from the crown of thorns worn by Jesus at his mock trial, which, when plunged into the soil, stating that his companions were "weary all", miraculously took root with leaves springing forth. The tree on "Wearyall Hill" is said to be the growth from that staff while a monastery stands in Glastonbury in his honor. [3]

It was during the Middle Ages that Joseph became a major saint and cult icon, and was proclaimed the ancestor of the British Monarchs. He is said to have brought with him a cup that, while supposedly used at the "Last Supper of Christ", was also said to have caught the blood of Jesus which dripped from the cross. It is this very cup that has long been believed, by many, to have been the illusive "Holy Grail".

These stories became a part of the Arthurian Grail legends during the Middle Ages, which have since prompted wide-spread interest and speculation. One legend suggests that Joseph hid the Grail at Chalice Well for safe keeping.[4] It is known that the Glastonbury Tor, where stands the roofless "Tower of St. Michael", the only remains of the church which once graced the hill, was a religious center for the Druids long before the day of Joseph. From a standpoint of interest, Tor is a Celtic word for "conical hill".[5]

Recent dowsing methods have now traced power lines in the earth. Glastonbury is said to be the center of four vortices, at which these magnetic leylines cross, producing great spiritual energy. These are located at the Tor, the ruins of the Lady Chapel Abby, Wearyall Hill, and the Chalice Well.[6]

Chapter 14 Footnotes

[1]Eden Communications. (2008). *Arimathea*.
Retrieved March 2008 from Web Bible
Encyclopedia located at
http://www.christiananswers.net/dictionary/arimath
ea.html
[2]Britannia.com. (2001). *Joseph of Arimathea*.
Retrieved March 2008 from
http://www.britannia.com/history/biographies/josep
h.html
[3]Ibid
[4]Ibid
[5]*Glastonbury Tor* retrieved from Wikipedia, the free
encyclopedia website located at
http://en.wikipedia.org/wiki/Glastonbury_Tor
[6]McMillan, Atasha. *Magical Mystery Tor: Legends,
folklore and strange experiences around
Glastonbury Tor*. Retrieved January 2008 from
http://www.glastonburytor.org.uk/mysterytor.html

**Joseph of Arimathea prepares Christ for burial
by Alexandre Bida (1874)**

Chapter Fifteen
The Samaritans

Most of the forth chapter of the Gospel attributed to St. John is taken up by the story of a woman whom Jesus meets at "Jacob's well" in Samaria. It is a fact that the Jews and the Samaritans had no known association. So much so, that this woman was suitably shocked that Jesus should ask her for a drink (v7). According to John, this was a purposeful action, on behalf of Jesus, to unify the Samaritans with his message and his mission. As a result of this act, many accepted him as the awaited messiah.

Who were the Samaritans? Why is that they were hated so badly by the Jews?

In 529 BC, when the Jews were released from Babylonian Captivity and allowed to return to their homeland, they found that their land was occupied by foreigners from other lands who had also been displaced by the conquering Assyrians and Babylonians.[1] In direct disobedience to the Jewish laws forbidding mixed marriage unions with pagans, many Israelites intermarried with these peoples.

The descendants of these marriages became outcasts in Israel, settling in the area known as Samaria, in northern Palestine, taking over lands previously allotted to the Tribe of Ephraim, already dispersed into other nations as a part of the "Ten Lost Tribes". In Jesus' day, Palestine was divided into three provinces: Galilee, Samaria, and Judea.[2] Samaria was in the center. Orthodox Jews would go many miles out of their way to detour past Samaria, so as not to come in contact with one of the inhabitants.

The prophets strongly condemned the Samaritans for wickedness, idolatry, immorality and oppression of the poor. By having no contact with them, many of whom were distant relations, they seemed to ignore, or chose not to believe, that many Samaritans kept holy the **Pentateuch** or **Torah** (the Jewish books of Law), accepted Moses as the true prophet, and worshiped the God of Israel.

Among sacred objects preserved to this day is the **Samaritan Pentateuch**, comprised of old Hebrew, or Phoenician script, similar to those letters in use before the Captivity. It is believed that this authentic scripture, in use as early as 681 BC[3], was preserved and utilized in Samaritan worship soon after their formation as a separate people.

Another illustration of Christian scripture is the parable of Jesus found in the Gospel of Luke 10:30-37, in which a Samaritan is used to exemplify good, attending to a man of Jerusalem, presumably a Jew, who had been robbed, stripped naked, beaten and left "half dead". Two pious Jews, a priest and another Levite, who should have been the prime example of righteousness, passed him by, deliberately crossing over to the other side of the road, ignoring his needs.

And finally, in the story of the ten lepers being cleansed, also related by Luke, Jesus made no difference in Jews and Samaritans. The only one who returned to give thanks was said to have been a Samaritan.[4]

By these very examples, Jesus grossly condemned prejudice, placing love at the heart of his message, further enraging the established religious leaders.

Chapter 15 Footnotes

[1]Pope, John A. (Ed.) (1988). Who Were the Samaritans? *Mysteries of the Bible* (p 206). Readers Digest Association: Pleasantville, NY.
[2]Lockyer, Herbert, Sr. (Ed.) (1986). Region of Samaria (p. 941). *The Liberty Illustrated Bible Dictionary*. Thomas Nelson Publishers: Nashville, TN.
[3]Ibid
[4]Luke 17:12-20

**The Arrival of the Good Samaritan at the Inn
by Gustave Dore**

Chapter Sixteen
The Writer of Hebrews

After 2,000 years, biblical scholars have yet to reach a conclusion as to the identity of the writer of the New Testament Epistle to the Hebrews. The author is nowhere identified in the content, and it is placed in the canon along with the letters of the Apostle Paul. John Calvin saw this as one of the most important books in the Bible.[1] Many have identified St. Paul as the most likely candidate, and up until the nineteenth century, the issue was not debated. Does this belief still hold true?

Those clinging to this argument cite the fact that, like Paul's writings, the Epistle to the Hebrews sets forth in glorious wording, the doctrine of the high priesthood of Jesus, placing his office as superior to the Levitical line of Aaron. However, with Jesus being of the tribe of Judah, this would have been a problem under Jewish tradition. It is in Hebrews 12:2, that the writer states Jesus as the author and perfecter of the faith. We know that Paul identified himself in all of the other epistles. If this is his work, why does he not do so here?

Not only is its authorship in question, but also its audience, according to scholars, in that the heading "To the Hebrews" is not found in the earliest known manuscripts. The closing[2] of "grace be with you all" hardly identifies a clear-cut audience.

Another problem with Pauline authorship is the place from which the scriptural quotations are taken. In his letters, St. Paul quotes from the original Masoretic Hebrew text of the *Tanakh*. In the letter identified as the Epistle to the Hebrews, these references come from the *Septuagint*.

One suggestion has been that it is a subscription of a sermon of Paul's by St. Luke, a doctor with a command of the Greek language, who may have used such quotations. Another possibility is Barnabas. Being a Levite, he may have had a reason to focus on the priesthood.

Martin Luther felt that Apollos, another educated and dedicated proponent and evangelist of the mission of Jesus as the Christ, may have been the author. Priscilla and Clement of Alexandria have also been suggested as possible candidates. According to Eusebius (c. 263-340), however, Clement (c. 150-215) taught that "Paul wrote the Hebrews in the Hebrew language and that Luke carefully translated it into Greek" which is a most intriguing theory.

The well-known answer of the famous Christian philosopher and scholar, Origen of Alexandria (c. 185-254),[3] when put the question of deeming who wrote this anonymous book, is "God only knows".[4]

Chapter 16 Footnotes

[1]Crampton, W. Gary, Dr. (2003). *Hebrews Who is the Author?* Retrieved March 2008 from http://www.fpcr.org/blue_banner_articles/Who-Wrote-Hebrews.htm in reference to John Calvin, *Commentaries*, XXII:xxvi

[2]Hebrews 13:35

[3]*Origen of Alexandria (185 – 254 AD).* Retrieved February 2008 from The Internet Encyclopedia of Philosophy website located at http://www.iep.utm.edu/o/origen.htm

[4]Schaff, Phillip. (1890). *NPNF2-01. Eusebius Pamphilius:Church History, Life of Constantine, Oration in Praise of Constantine* (p 273). Christian Literature Publishing Company: New York, NY. Retrieved March 2008 from http://www.ccel.org/ccel/schaff/npnf201.iii.xi.xxv.html in reference to Eusebius, Historia Ecclesiastica (Ecclesiastical   History) 6.25

Chapter Seventeen
John the Revelator

In Hebrew, John (יוֹחָנָן, *Yôhānnān*) means "the Lord (Yahweh) is merciful", a name that was not an uncommon name in first century Judea, any more than it is in English speaking countries in its present form today. John the Revelator, or John of Patmos, is believed by the majority of Christian scholars to be one and the same with St. John, the Apostle.[1]

He is accredited with writing the Gospel of John, I, II and III John, and the book titled *The Revelation of Jesus Christ*, the final book in the Christian canon of scripture or New Testament.

One problem with some in accepting this teaching is the fact that the author of different books is known by different names. The author of the Gospel of John and I John is referred to as *John the Theologian* and *John the Evangelist*. The author of II and III John is officially recognized by the council at Rome as *John the Presbyter*. The writer of the Book of the Revelation is strictly known as *John the Divine*, or *John of Patmos*, the book in question being formally called, by the Roman Church, *"The Apocalypse of St. John the Divine"*, "Apocalypse" being Greek for Revelation.[2]

While all five books show similarities in theological background, they do contain specific differences. This fact also causes further debate as to authorship; in fact, II John was officially regarded as being the work of a separate author by the Council at Rome in 382 under Pope Damascus.[3]

In the Gospel accounts, John the Apostle is stated as being the son of Zebedee, brother to the Apostle James (not to be confused with the brother of Jesus). His mother was likely Salome. These brothers were referred to by Jesus as "sons of thunder".[4] The most critical of scholars even question his authorship of the Gospel attributed to him, placing the time of the final edition as the late first or early second century, even though Jesus, on the cross, is quoted as placing his mother into John's hands ("the disciple whom he loved").[5]

Since the discovery of the *Dead Sea Scrolls* at Qumran, for some, Johannine scholarship has taken a change. Several hymns, said to have originated in the community of the Essenes, containing similar metaphors (light and dark, truth and lies, etc.), are also found in the Gospel attributed to John. Many have felt that John the Baptist fit the mold of an Essene prophet, with some believing that the Apostle John was originally a follower of the Baptist.

Eusebius of Caesarea (c. 275–339), also known as Eusebius Pamphilia, often called the father of church history, because of his early work in its recording[6], clearly stated that two different Johns must be distinguished, John the Apostle, and John the Presbyter, quoting from Papias, an early saint of the church from the first half of the first century, whom Eusebius called, "Bishop of Hierapolis" (part of modern Turkey).[7]

Papias, relying on the tradition upheld in Ephesus, where John the Apostle reputedly lived, while witnessing Ireneus, a disciple of Polycarp, in the second generation after the Apostle, stated emphatically that John the Apostle was the author of the Gospel attributed to him.[8] Since the discoveries of the various Gnostic texts, there have been critics of this view. However, this statement, as well as the texts of the recently discovered *Rylands Library Papyrus (P52)*, dated at 100-175 AD, as to the spread of the Gospel of John in Egypt, coupled with the statement of Clement of Alexandria that John the Apostle "inspired by the Holy Spirit...wrote a spiritual Gospel"[9], are good testimony to this creed.

Clement also saw the Apostle as the author of Revelation, as did Justin Martyr (100-165), in his *Dialogue with Tryphon*.

Yet, there are scholars, today, who argue that they view authorship of any books by John the Apostle, the brother of Zebedee, as being highly unlikely, stating that he was an "unlettered man".[10] Some have even attributed the Gospel of John to Mary Magdalene, as was implied in the Gnostic gospel believed to bear her name.

Although most still hold fast to apostolic authorship, stating that both his missionary journeys in Asia and the authority of the text make him the ideal candidate, "The Revelation of Jesus Christ" may have been written by another John.

It is impossible to be certain. It may well be that the writer of the Apocalypse never lived and died in Ephesus. The only fact of surety is that this John was banished to the Isle of Patmos for his faith, and by his testimony did proclaim to "bear record of the word of God, and the testimony of Jesus Christ, and all things that he saw"[11] pronouncing his blessing in the next verse on those who read, and kept "the things which are written therein, for the time is at hand".

Originally a disputed book for inclusion in the canon[12], most traditional theologians view the Book of Revelation, itself, as purely symbolic, feeling that its writing was triggered by the resentment of both Jews and Christians to the continuing Roman domination during the early church years. While symbolism obviously prevails in its awesome references to horsemen, beasts, heavenly signs, and sounding of trumps, there are millions around the world who believe that there is yet to be a somewhat literal fulfillment to its startling prophecies.

Chapter 17 Footnotes

[1]*John the Apostle* retrieved March 3008 from Wikipedia, the free encyclopedia website located at http://en.wikipedia.org/wiki/John_the_apostle
[2]Ibid
[3]*Authorship of the Johannine Works* retrieved March 2008 from Wikipedia, the free encyclopedia website located at http://en.wikipedia.org/wiki/Authorship_of_the_Johannine_Works
[4]Matthew 3:17
[5]John 19:26, 27
[6] *Eusebius of Caesarea* retrieved March 2008 from Wikipedia, the free encyclopedia website located at http://en.wikipedia.org/wiki/Eusebius_of_Caesarea
[7]*Papias* retrieved March 2008 from Wikipedia, the free encyclopedia website located atehttp://en.wikipedia.org/wiki/Papias
[8]Papias, *Testimony of Irenaeus* retrieved March 2008 from http://hajimac.qee.jp/papiase.htm
[9]*Authorship of the Johannine Works* retrieved March 2008 from Wikipedia, the free encyclopedia website located at http://en.wikipedia.org/wiki/Authorship_of_the_Johannine_Works, Reference to *Quis dives salvabitur* 42,1
[10]Pope, John A. (Ed.) (1994). John. *Who's Who In The Bible* (p 233). Readers Digest Association: Pleasantville, NY.
[11]Revelation 1:2, KJV
[12]Tobin, Paul N. *The New Testament Canon.*

Retrieved March 2008 from Rejection of Pascal's
Wager: A Skeptic's Guide to Christianity website
located at
http://www.geocities.com/paulntobin/ntcanon.html

The Four Horsemen of the Apocalypse
by Albrecht Druer

Appendix

Index of Illustrations

Ancient Texts Mentioned and/or Referenced Within Text of Book

Direct Biblical References and/or Quotes

Old Testament

Book	Chapter/Verse	Page
Genesis		
	2:21-24, 4:8, 16	8
	4:17	9
	3:20, 5:4	11
	1:28	12
	1:2	18
	1:1	21
	6:1,2, 4	29
	6	32, 35, 36
	6:1-4	38
	11:16, 24	48
	36:33	52
	36:4, 11	49
	25:1, 2, 5	50
	10:29	51
	19:1, 21:1	58
	11:32, 12:1,2, 15:1	123
	15:5, 16, 17:1-11	124, 125
	17:15-22	125
	16	126
Exodus		
	21:6	30
	2:10	71
	1:11	72
Leviticus		
	20:27	92

Numbers

13:33	81

Deuteronomy

3:11	80, 81, 83
3:13	81
1:28	82

Joshua

10:1	59
1:1	87
2:8-10	89

Judges

10:12	20
18	134

I Samuel

28:3, 4, 5	92
28:7-20	92, 93, 94
28:1-4, 31	95
28:12, 15, 16	97
1:1, 19	159

II Samuel

5:11	107

I Kings

6:1	72
10:1-13	101-103
7:13, 5:1-10	108
17:6	130

I Chronicles

5:26	130

II Chronicles

2:13	108
2:12	109

Job

1:6-12	33
2:1	36
29:25	47
32	48
1:1	49
26:1-32:5, 29:25	50
28:21	50
19:23-29	51

Psalms

82:6	31
110:4	56

Isaiah

14:12-15	32

Daniel

3:25-28	36

Hebrews

	7:1-8	57
	11:29	89
	13:25	169

James

	2:25	89

II Peter

	2:4, 5	38

Jude

	6	38

Revelation

	1:2	175

Micmac Hieroglyphs wre already in use before 1738 when the Abbe Maillard adopted them for his *Manuel Hieroglyphique Micmac* the ancient Egyptian equivalent signs were not deciphered until 1823. The same hieroglyphs for silver and for gold as were used by the ancient Egyptians.

Meaning	Micmac	Ancient Egyptian	Meaning	Micmac	Ancient Egyptian
Name			Men		
Mountains			Ram, sheep		
Metal			Mouth		
Silver			to walk or motion		
Gold			Flowing		
Stone			to become		
Sand, dust			and, also		
Sea, lake			out of, from		
River			them, their to them		
To be like			I, my, me		
Idols			Thou, thee		

This page and the next are taken from *"Beyond Any Shadow of Doubt"*, a document prepared by British historian Niven Sinclair for use in a video presentation, showing striking proofs of Pre-Columbian Atlantic Crossings, leading up to that of Prince

Henry St. Clair in 1398. The video was released for use by Clan Sinclair. The Clan in Canada published it in *Roslin O Roslin* in the spring and summer 1996 issues. Used by permission. The charts may need magnification for better clarity.

As the modern decipherment of Egyptian began only in 1797, when Zoega deduced the meaning "name" for the cartouche sign, it is evident that the Micmac hieroglyphs must already have been transmitted to North America more than 2000 years ago, when they were still in use in Egypt.

Meaning	Micmac	Ancient Egyptian	Meaning	Micmac	Ancient Egyptian
Reed, grass			Today, now		
To keep safe or preserve			Water, rain		
Greetings, hello			Dwelling, santuary		
Shining, glory			Earth or lower world		
Rock-slab			Heaven		
Not			Burn to ashes		
Make an offering			Fire		
Tremble, earthquake			To skip about, leap		
Come in haste			Faults, sins		
Full, all			Fruit		

Notes

Notes

Notes

www.ingramcontent.com/pod-product-compliance
Lightning Source LLC
Chambersburg PA
CBHW022129080426
42734CB00006B/283